From Hollow to HOPE

© 2024 by CAM Books, a wholly owned, for-profit subsidiary of Christian Aid Ministries, Berlin, Ohio.

All rights reserved. No part of this book may be reproduced or stored in any retrieval system, in any form or by any means, electronic or mechanical, without written permission from the publisher except for brief quotations embodied in critical articles and reviews.

ISBN: 978-1-63813-381-0

Cover and interior design: Kristi Yoder

Printed in the USA

Published by:

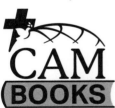

CAM Books
P.O. Box 355
Berlin, Ohio 44610 USA
Phone: 330.893.4828
Fax: 330.893.4893
cambooks.org

From Hollow to Hope

One woman's struggle
with an eating disorder—
and how God can heal
us from obsessions.

Sarah Weaver and Hannah Martin

From stark despair to hope and healing, Sarah takes us along on her journey with God. Hannah's additional information and probing questions help make this book a powerful tool.

    Learn to delight in the gift of food—enough, but not too much.

—*Ernest & Yvonne Witmer*

A compelling, heart-probing journey of loosening bondage and finding freedom in the loving heart of our Father, where the Truth sets us FREE.

—*Cleason & Dawn Sensenig, ministry and board members at Stories Made New*

From Hollow to Hope reveals the hidden side of eating disorders and the mental, emotional, and spiritual conditions that lead to them. The author's personal experience demonstrates that recovery and healing are possible.

—*Chadwick & Rebecca McMurray*

Contents

Preface vii
Introduction xi
Prologue xv

Part One: Taking Control 21
1. A Distorted View 23
2. Roots of Fear 31
3. Learning to Cope 39

Part Two: Out of Control 49
4. No Pain—No Gain 51
5. The Lie 61
6. One Girl—Two Lives 71
7. Dragged Back From the Cliff 81

Part Three: Grasping for Control 91
8. A Glimmer of Hope 93
9. Hidden Rooms 103
10. You Cannot Get Around It 117
11. Who Am I? 125

Part Four: Surrendering Control 133
12. Waiting on the Lord 135
13. What About Anger? 149
14. Reactions 163

Part Five: Under God's Control 171
15. Swapping My Bondage 173
16. Sorting It Out 179
17. Backwards Freedom 185
18. A New Gauge 193
19. Try It MY Way 199
20. Straight Talk 207
21. Letter of Release 211
22. Healed? 215
    Closing Letter 223
    Resources 225

Preface

As you step into the pages of this book, my prayer is that you will find hope and healing in whatever journey you are on. Life is full of difficulties. Day by day we face many choices, some of which have lasting consequences.

This is a true story, my story, of a conservative Anabaptist woman who has walked through the difficulties of an eating disorder and found healing and hope.

An eating disorder was my labeled struggle, but the purpose of this book is not to highlight that part of my life. The goal is far greater—to bring honor and glory to the Great Physician. I've allowed myself to be vulnerable through the leading of God so He can highlight His purpose for all His children who are in any kind of pain or struggle.

As you read, place your own battle alongside mine. Let God show you who He wants you to be. I encourage you to read not only my story but also Hannah's insights as a study guide to go with it. Let God speak to you through the encouragement of her words.

When this life's battles are over, I pray we will meet on the other side. All of us who have been redeemed will remain forever by the throne of God, serving Him day and night. There will be no more pain or hunger or thirst. "For the Lamb which is in the midst of the throne shall feed them, and shall lead them unto living fountains of waters: and God shall wipe away all tears from their eyes" (Revelation 7:17).

Be strong,
Sarah

When God walked Sarah into my life, I knew who she was, but I didn't know her personally. What started as a connection over our common interest in writing soon became a deeper sharing of the healing God had done in my life. As I opened up my story and a friendship developed, Sarah started giving glimpses of a desperate search for healing in her life. I knew she had struggled with an eating disorder in her past but was unaware that it was still a deeply hidden reality.

As we touched the surface issues of depression and emotional struggles, God brought the eating disorder glaringly to the forefront in a way that could not be ignored. God not only worked in Sarah's heart but also showed me areas in my own life that needed a deeper touch from Him.

The shaded parts throughout this book, usually labeled "Mentor's Thoughts," are mine, written to round out Sarah's story with facts, perspective, and resources. There are also questions to use as a study guide for anyone seeking freedom from bondage.

> My prayer is that you, dear reader, can come to a deeper understanding of the challenges you face in your life, and that God can use your broken places to show His heart to others.
>
> Come along as we walk through a journey of healing.
>
> Hannah

We authors have chosen to use pen names to protect our families and children. However, if readers really want to know, they can learn our true identities. It wasn't because of shame or a desire to hide that we are withholding our identity, but to respect and give those closest to us anonymity. If anyone should wish to contact the authors, feel free to do so through the publisher.

Thank you and may God bless you and draw you near to His heart through the pages of this book.

Hannah & Sarah

Introduction

Heart's Cry

"I'm so tired, Lord. This feels so intense . . . Will it always be this way?"

The tears made a steady trickle down my cheeks as I continued my walk along our beautiful country road. The sobs finally dissipated, and I walked on with a heart aching for peace. It had been a difficult day, and I sensed a mental and spiritual tiredness beyond what I wanted to handle.

Looking up into the sky, I spoke to the One who has done so much for me—more than anyone else ever has or will. "God," I prayed, "I am yours. Use me in whatever way you choose. Help me be faithful and sincere. I am yours."

A breath of a breeze touched my face and seemed to linger on the tears. I couldn't describe it, but I understood it completely. It was not audible and not intense or overwhelming.

Nothing changed around me, but I sensed a breath from heaven, a whisper . . . "Go and tell them. Warn them. Will you tell them for me?"

It wasn't words as much as Spirit language. I felt a moving in the deepest part of my soul. "I want you to tell them . . ."

Tears streaming down my cheeks, I raised my face toward the sky. I didn't understand what it meant or what I was agreeing to, but I answered from the depths of my soul, "I will, Lord. I will do whatever it takes to tell them. Show me how, Lord."

Something inside me immediately kicked in with doubts and fears. *How might this look or be interpreted? What will people say?*

But if you have ever heard that Spirit voice—you will understand. *I have to tell them.*

May God use the pages of this book, the vulnerability of my story, to "tell them."

"Will You Tell Them for Me?"

"Why must I share the dark, the pain?
It's my battle, my shame.
Why should I open wide my heart?
Expose this ruthless game?

"Who am I? I fail every day;
I've nothing I can give.
How dare I show the hopelessness
Of the choices I have lived?

"Why me? Why must I be the one?
Surely another can.
I've enough to do to fight each day;
This cannot be the plan."

Listen…He speaks,
And to my knees I fall in sudden tears.
"What if I've brought you to this place,
And through all these years…

"What if it's part of your healing…
The way to truly mend?
Dear child, I ask you, take your pain
And go warn all of them.

"Go tell them about Satan's scheme;
His distractions, his ploy,
And how he'll pull them farther in
Until he steals their joy."

Weeping, I ask yet one more time,
"Lord, truly must it be me?
I'm not sure I can do it right
To actually help them see."

He doesn't say another word…
But slowly His hands spread wide.
I see the wounds He bore for me—
The scar upon His side.

How can I not do as He asks?
For all He's done for me?
"I'll tell them, God. I'll share my pain,
If through it YOU they'll see."

—Sarah

Hidden Signs

I leaned forward to get a better look at the picture. To the untrained eye, it was a nice picture of sisters smiling into the camera.

I looked for the signs I was told were there. "In this picture you can see bruising on my arm…I was basically only drinking water. I hardly remember that weekend because I could barely keep myself alert and focused. My hips hurt because I wore a belt around my waist, and it chafed because I pulled it so tight…I had open sores that wouldn't heal."

Introduction

What would cause a person to get to this point? Paul tells us in Ephesians 5:29, "For no man ever yet hated his own flesh; but nourisheth and cherisheth it." And yet, in the darkness of an eating disorder, there is such a fervent hatred for the body that desperate measures are taken to bring it under subjection—even if it means a brush with death. Inner emotional pain is taken out in physically abusing one's body. Dark thoughts inside the mind take on a voice that is harsh and relentless in its demands for ever more severe methods to reach unattainable goals.

What stood out most in the photograph were the dark circles around empty eyes. Eyes that had lost hope. Eyes that testified to a battle that consumed every moment. The smile distracted from the truth the eyes couldn't hide.

One of the strongest characteristics of an eating disorder is the desperate need for secrecy. It is what keeps a person in bondage even when others reach out to help. The voice inside threatens and cajoles. It warns of dire consequences if the secret is found out. It promises perfection and peace if only its demands are met.

It is never quiet.

If that is you, my friend, don't despair—there is hope! The God of all peace can and will heal. But it is not an easy road or a short one. It is a journey.

It is taking one step at a time—guided by the Great Liberator.

Prologue

A Jolt of Auschwitz

Look at them... That's how you want to look... You want to be that thin.

Trying to ignore the thoughts, I turned the page. Bile rose in my throat as I fought the condemnation while wrapped in shame.

The thoughts hit hard. *You are totally pathetic. Those people are starving...*

I couldn't get the picture out of my head... A group of men dressed in rags, cheekbones protruding, ribcages showing...

True to the era, it was a grainy black-and-white photo—but it may as well have been in vibrant colors. The dullness of the picture didn't dim its effect on me. It lured me to look... and to keep looking.

Bones... stretched skin... large, haunted eyes.

I immediately recognized the oily feeling. Anxiety caused my adrenaline to spike as I dragged my eyes away.

Auschwitz.

So much pain and unimaginable suffering is linked to this concentration camp that no matter how many years roll by, it cannot be forgotten. The horror of those days still lives as the blood of the innocent cries from the ground. The book I was holding was laced from cover to cover with millions of tears.

Jolted to reality, I covered my eyes with my hands.

How dare my mind react positively to these pictures? It was horribly shameful to see something so dreadfully sad—and yet recognize feelings of longing.

How dare my mind betray me like this?

And then the thoughts of condemnation came, so common after over twenty years of existence.

You are horrible… What a loser… and so out of control. Look at how fat you are! You know you're not allowed to eat… See? Those men are how you should look.

No. I won't listen.

My arms tingled as I struggled to fight the anxiety and fear. I had learned how to quiet the thoughts… the voices of hate. I thought of Isaiah 59:19: "So shall they fear the name of the LORD from the west, and his glory from the rising of the sun. When the enemy shall come in like a flood, the Spirit of the LORD shall lift up a standard against him."

I'm in recovery, I reminded myself. *It's been almost two years now. There is nothing there anymore—nothing to go back to.* The only way to drown out the thoughts was to replace them with truths that could not be changed or argued against.

Even though I was in recovery, my "Auschwitz" was still all too familiar. The bondage, the razor wire, the screaming words were much the same.

Trapped in an eating disorder, there are throngs of people in prisons as tightly controlled as a guarded concentration camp. But there is one great difference: the Jews couldn't escape because of the guards, while eating disorder victims are held hostage only by a mind that believes it cannot escape. People caught in an eating disorder are walking skeletons who have been misled to believe this is the way to peace and happiness. Bones, stretched skin, and aching hunger have become a misguided source of perverse joy—a semblance of control.

I know, because I was one of them.

Though bound up tightly and so controlled, I would have argued vehemently that the prison was not even there. I was just fine, thank you, and I didn't need rescuing.

I have now found hope—real hope—in the Redeemer of all prisoners. He is the only One who can cut the razor wire, stop the screaming madness, and break the bonds to freedom. He paid a price so high it cost His life.

Jesus Christ.

Let me share what He has done for me...

Seeking the Lost

I couldn't find my phone.

I was working in the kitchen and thought of a call I needed to make, but my phone was not where I usually put it. *Where could it be?*

I searched the kitchen thoroughly and checked both bathrooms. No phone. I knew the ringer and vibrator were both turned off, so it wouldn't help to call it. This was frustrating. How could my phone just disappear?

I slowed down and thought it through. *When did I last use the phone?* Mentally I retraced my steps that morning... *The basement freezer!* I had been to the freezer to get some corn, and that was the last time I remembered using the phone.

Sure enough. There it was, on the shelf with the jars of peaches—right where I had put it when I needed two hands to dig into the freezer. When logic had failed to find it, tracing back through events had done the trick.

Far too many of us find ourselves midway through life when we discover that something vital has been lost. For someone who has faced betrayal and deep hurts, it may be trust that is lost. For the small girl who has lost her innocence at the hands of others, it may be her sense of self-worth. For children dealing with painful emotions brought on by difficult circumstances, it may be hope that is lost.

Childhood trauma of any kind, if not dealt with, will cause a loss of trust, self-worth, and hope.

When a child, like Sarah, concludes that she is unable to trust anyone, she withdraws her heart and builds walls of protection around it. Many times this is a silent, hidden process that can be missed even by close family members. Negative voices slowly take control and tell her she must not let anyone in too close. The voices tell her she is worthless, unlovable, and unwanted. They tell her there is no use trying to change because it will always be this way; there is no hope. The longer it goes, the higher, stronger, and thicker those walls become. A piece of her heart is locked away—and with it, the ability to feel emotions in a healthy way.

When God comes knocking on those heart-walls, it is a long and painful process to allow Him to tear them down. It is like peeling back the layers of an onion...one layer at a time and not too fast. And just as working with onions produces tears, allowing God to dismantle the walls around our heart will produce many, many tears of healing.

Often this healing process will not look logical to others, especially to those who have not experienced similar trauma.

Going beyond logic, we must allow God to peel back the layers in the order they were created. There are layers of rejection, confusion, shame—and beneath it all, fear.

How can these layers of pain and fear be understood? How can we know what steps to take toward freedom?

To find something, we must go back to the place where it was lost.

For my phone, it meant backtracking through the events of my morning to where I had last used it. In a wounded life, it means searching back through the layers of pain to find the root. How were trust, self-worth, and hope lost? Where did fear first take root?

Come along as we look back through events that shaped the thick walls surrounding a young heart—one that was so afraid…

Part One

Taking Control

The struggle for control began in the Garden of Eden when Satan convinced Eve that God was withholding the best from them. Through Adam and Eve's choice to disobey God's direct command, sin and death entered the world. Ever since then, each of us faces the same struggle. Can we trust God's will and direction for our lives, or will we take the reins of control for ourselves?

The root of an eating disorder is anchored in the decision (deliberate or not) to control our world according to our own rules. When we do this, we believe the same lies that deceived Adam and Eve.

In Part One, we follow Sarah's painful journey of fear, shame, and self-hatred to the place of decision—the choice to take control.

chapter 1

A Distorted View

My cheeks blushed crimson. I felt so ashamed.

I walked away from the scale and back to my desk. *Why does the teacher have to put our weight on a chart for everyone to see?* My number wasn't the highest, but it wasn't the lowest either.

I glanced at one of my classmates whose number was lower than mine. She grinned at me. *She thinks I'm fat.* I looked at some of the other children in our classroom. They were also grinning at me. My heart sank lower and lower.

I blinked back tears and ducked behind my desktop, trying to hide my blushing face. The health book I had loved so much now made me feel sick to my stomach. *I am fat.* The thought mortified me.

Everything the teacher said next about healthy foods and fattening foods made me feel more like crying. I swallowed hard. I liked candy…and cookies…and ice cream…My mom and dad had never told me they were bad. I felt horrible inside.

Maybe Mom and Dad don't want me to know. Maybe they are ashamed of me too. Maybe my teacher also thinks I am fat. And the other children. That's why they are laughing at me.

I glanced at the row of numbers on the board. My number hadn't changed. *I hate this.*

"Please write your height and weight into your health book," the teacher said. I could hardly see the page because of the tears that filled my eyes. My cheeks burned with shame.

I wanted to hide. I didn't understand everything going on inside me. I just knew I was ashamed. Very ashamed.

I was in second grade.

I tried not to look, but I couldn't help it.

As the voice of the minister droned on, my young mind was elsewhere. I was sitting in a row of little girls on the front benches of our red brick church when I suddenly noticed something.

My legs are way bigger than all the rest. Looking down the row of girls, I became hot. *I'm fat.*

The realization hit me hard. A sinking feeling settled in the pit of my stomach. It was a feeling that was becoming all too familiar.

Shame.

A smaller girl sat just down the row. *She doesn't have big legs. She is skinny. Why can't I look like her?*

I thought of my older sister. *She is older than I am, but I am taller…And fatter.*

I felt sick. Yucky. *I'm fat. I'm not a nice girl. People don't like me.*

A great sadness overwhelmed me. My heart hurt, and I didn't understand why. *It must be because I am fat…*

These are some of my earliest memories. Looking back now, I wonder why it affected me so much. Why would a young child react in such a devastating way to something that shouldn't be that important, something so benign?

I never told anyone. Maybe if I had shared these feelings with my mom, she could have told me that height has something to do with weight. She could have explained that everyone is built differently—that genetics play a role, and that God made me the way I am. Maybe she could have pointed out the truth—that I was not fat but just tall and big for my age. And that I come from a family that is not petite.

Maybe she could have explained what I now know—that foods are not bad in themselves. Maybe if I had confided in her and let the tears flow, she would have seen how deeply the other children's grins affected me. Then she could have explained that possibly they weren't laughing at me at all. Maybe I had interpreted it wrong. Maybe they were just as unsure and ashamed as I was, and they just grinned because they were my friends.

My mom would have cared. I see that now. But then... as a small child, I just didn't talk about it. I kept everything inside, tightly covered. It became a way of life. As time passed, these faulty thinking patterns continued to grow. They became deep-rooted hurts in my heart and mind, growing until they were monsters of distortion.

As we look back to our childhood years, there will be memories we don't care to think about. We all have them. But these memories, no matter how painful, are real. And they continue to shape us as adults.

If not dealt with, childhood trauma can lead to deep-seated feelings of shame or worthlessness. The pain or emotional trauma "freezes" in time, becoming entrenched. Though a child's body grows and develops, the inner feelings and thoughts stay tucked away, never able to come to maturity or understanding of the truth. The foundation of distorted beliefs and faulty thinking patterns remains firmly in place.

That is why we go back.

> For every distorted childhood view, God has a beautiful truth to show us.

We go back to our earliest memories not to place blame, but to see where our thought train came from—and where it got stuck. We also want to identify *why* our viewpoint became distorted.

Although childhood memories may seem insignificant to some, for me they bring tears as I write. They are not tears of frustration or anger or blame, but tears of sadness—a great, aching sadness. A sadness that my faulty, deep-rooted beliefs shaped so much of my life.

Sadness, because of the fallen world in which we live. Sadness, because though all Christian parents desire the best for their children, not a single parent is perfect. Sadness, because too many children grow up and turn against their parents, blaming them for their problems, when that isn't the answer at all. Sadness, because as adults, too many of us are only stunted little people walking around in grown-up bodies, our minds and emotions still stuck in immature thinking.

There are all kinds of stories—all kinds of ways we can become distorted and stunted in our views and thinking. But regardless of the situation, no matter how painful, it is not the end of the story. For every distorted childhood view, God has a beautiful truth to show us.

With God, we can walk back in our memories and let Him show us the truth. With Him, we can think about and explore those memories that still cause pain. One memory at a time, God will help us see every circumstance through adult eyes instead of the stunted childhood view. He can lead us to a mature understanding that brings lasting peace and freedom.

God was there with me in school. He was with me in church. He was with me in every memory I can think of, even if it involves a twisted viewpoint. In every circumstance, He was there.

How do I know?

Because of the words of Jesus Himself, "Lo, I am with you alway, even unto the end of the world. Amen" (Matthew 28:20).

Amen. No exceptions. He is God, and He always was and always is. He's here now, and He was there then.

Like untangling a rope, we go back to where the tangle formed, then we can start to unravel the lies and bring in truth. God can take our distorted views and change them into something He can use for His glory.

One memory at a time.

Mentor's Thoughts

Children with obsessive-compulsive tendencies are highly susceptible to distorted beliefs. Such children are very sensitive, prone to anxiety, and tend to internalize things instead of expressing them. They usually have perfectionist tendencies. Children with this temperament are especially vulnerable to eating disorders.

As in Sarah's case, the root may be a misperception of being fat—or at least fatter than other children their age. Maybe it was a word overheard and misunderstood. Maybe it was the unkind words of another child or the thoughtlessness of a sibling who mentioned something about being fat. This can be traumatizing whether or not there really is a weight problem.

Not all eating disorders start with a distorted view of being fat, but there is usually some negative perception. Maybe the child feels ugly, dumb, or like a loser. These misperceptions can become foundational beliefs that cause feelings of shame.

It is easy for parents to miss these distorted beliefs. And once detected, it can be difficult to know how to handle them wisely. Parents should watch for anxiety and teach their children how to deal with it. They should be careful not to be so critical that the children think they must be perfect to be accepted. The children should know their parents love them for who they are, not for what they do.

Sometimes there is blame to be placed for getting a vulnerable child off track, but many times there is not. My focus here is not to point fingers, but to create an awareness of what can go on inside a child's mind. For parents, please be careful—be vigilant. And most of all, make your home a safe place for your children to share their thoughts and fears.

> Children should know their parents love them for who they are, not for what they do.

Parents should be especially aware of perfectionist tendencies. Children with this personality trait struggle greatly with flexibility and openness. It affects their whole life and also has an effect on others. If not managed, it can lead to all kinds of emotional problems.

If your child struggles with this—or you yourself—there is a way to overcome it! There are ways to counteract those feelings and urges. That is why this book was written. Our ultimate goal is not just to triumph over perfectionism and obsessions, but to point to Christ as the only way to true freedom.

Writing Out Your Thoughts[1]...

1. Were there times when you were scared or sad, and you wondered if God really cared? Do you remember praying for Jesus to be with you but not feeling like He heard? Looking back now, can you see that He was with you?

2. Describe yourself as a child. How did you see yourself? Describe how you think you looked and acted. Also describe how you felt inside. Did you feel like other people loved and accepted you, or did you feel like you were a nuisance or unlovable? Be honest.

3. How was your experience as a child different from Sarah's? What did you believe about yourself that brought shame? Can you see how these negative beliefs were not rooted in truth?

4. Study the verse at the bottom. What does it tell you about how God feels about you? What does He promise to do for you?

> *Fear not: for I have redeemed thee, I have called thee by thy name; thou art mine. When thou passest through the waters, I will be with thee; and through the rivers, they shall not overflow thee: when thou walkest through the fire, thou shalt not be burned; neither shall the flame kindle upon thee. For I am the Lord thy God, the Holy One of Israel, thy Saviour.* Isaiah 43:1-3

---

[1] We recommend copying these questions into a notebook bought especially for this purpose, allowing plenty of room for your answers.

chapter 2

Roots of Fear

I wonder...

Why, as a small child, I was petrified of thunderstorms.

It was not just a subtle fear but a terror I cannot explain. There was a time it consumed me.

I got up in the morning thinking about the weather, terrified that we might have a thunderstorm. I don't know why or exactly when it started. Did we have a scary storm? Did I hear a story about a storm that made me afraid?

I really don't know.

Maybe it was because being in the barn during a storm didn't feel safe. Not all the windows were secure, and the barn seemed too exposed. Several times sparks traveled along the water lines during a lightning storm, and the cows got shocked. Maybe I was afraid the huge pine tree in front of our house would come crashing down—right into my bedroom.

Whatever it was, I had an unreasonable fear of thunderstorms. But I never felt comfortable sharing my fear. No one else seemed to be afraid, and I didn't want them to laugh at me.

But oh, how I prayed.

I would pray while I fed the calves, then check the horizon. Then I prayed while feeding the heifers—before checking the horizon again.

Anxiety filled me until I felt sick. We could see storms coming for quite a distance, and that in itself filled me with fear. At the first sign of dark clouds, my heart picked up its pace.

We had a weather radio, and Dad often listened to the weather forecast at the breakfast table. If thunderstorms were predicted for the afternoon or evening, I was on pins and needles all day. Sometimes I looked for a chance to listen to the forecast by myself, trying to find out if storms were on the way.

> A fear shared is half the fear.

Although it was irrational, I was petrified. It became a fear that consumed me. It also filled me with shame. *Why am I so afraid of thunderstorms? Other people aren't.* But I didn't know what to do about it.

Why didn't I tell someone? I guess that was also a fear, because I never said a word.

There were certain triggers. On a breezy, mild day, I would be just fine. But if we had no storms for a while, I became leery, knowing that sooner or later it was bound to happen. I would grow more and more wary and anxious.

By the time the next storm arrived, the fear would overwhelm me.

I wonder…

Why fear haunted me at night as I lay awake with snatches of the minister's sermon floating through my head—words about heaven and hell, and sin and salvation. I didn't understand them, and they made me afraid. Was it the same fear that made me look at the moon to see if it was red like blood, fearful that "the great day of the Lord" was near?

I wonder...

Why I had such a numbing fear that someone in my family would die. My heart was so gripped with fear at the thought that I prayed and prayed for God to take me home first.

I wonder...

What it would have been like to share those fears. What if I had been open enough to talk instead of chewing on my fingernails until they bled?

Why didn't I?

I don't know. Some of these questions may never have answers.

I wonder...

What fear would look like now, as an adult, if I had learned how to handle it as a child.

Would the things that still scare me and rob me of my peace be easier to deal with? If the things that cause me to tremble with anxiety could just be out in the open and understood, would they eventually go away?

I wonder...

What would happen if I could learn to express my fears immediately, both to people I trust and to my heavenly Father, the One who knows my thoughts better than I do myself. What if I simply dumped it all out when something causes me fear and anxiety? What if I immediately took every "thunderstorm" in my life to the One who made me?

I don't need to wonder anymore...because I know! I have discovered a wonderful truth:

A fear shared is half the fear.

Mentor's Thoughts

Fear is an emotion God designed for our protection. As a child, we learn to fear heights, wild animals, fire that is out of control, strangers that may hurt us, and many other things that could harm us. These are healthy fears. They are things to respect and treat with proper caution, but we should not be paralyzed by them.

Normal childhood trauma is something that cannot be avoided. Houses burn, people die, storms cause damage, bad things happen. Even messages in church about hell can bring fear into a young, immature mind that cannot discern the difference between godly admonitions and dire threats of eternal damnation. This is where loving, concerned parents can make a big difference. If parents talk about what was preached so children can understand it on their own level, it takes away the looming fear of things they cannot comprehend.

If children are left alone to process events too traumatic to understand, their fear is likely to grow and can become an unreasonable, paralyzing fear. It becomes more than their young minds can handle. To prevent this, children need someone to walk through their fears with them. They can usually remain emotionally undamaged if there are adults to provide a sense of safety and well-being—someone to help process the pain and fear.

But what if a child doesn't share or refuses to share?

There are a number of reasons why children fail to share their struggles. Sometimes the adults around them are not safe or may even be the source of the danger. Other times it is simply that children are afraid or unwilling to share their feelings and worries. They may be especially uncomfortable about exposing their fears.

When children keep their fears locked up, they can become captive of fears that petrify them. These children may live with hidden fears that even well-meaning adults are unaware of. Over time, these fears become larger than life and more and more carefully hidden from those around them. These hidden fears can become entrenched in a child's life and cause physical, emotional, and mental disorders until they are unlocked and dealt with as an adult.

Growing Up Inside

Many of us remember having trust issues with our parents. I often felt that my mother didn't understand me, and that my dad had no idea how I felt. This caused a lack of trust in sharing my heart. Sometimes my mom was busy when I was trying to share something important, only half listening to what probably sounded like just more of my constant chattering. Her inattention, however, hurt me and caused me to block her out of my confidence. I thought she didn't care, and the hurt went deep.

> Children need someone to walk through their fears with them.

As I grew up, my outlook matured, and eventually I found myself in my mother's shoes—with chattering children of my own. And just like my mother, in the busyness of life, sometimes I did not hear a little heart that needed love and attention. It was then that I could revisit the old, hidden hurts and see them through the eyes of an adult.

My parents really did care, but they never realized how much my little heart was hurt by their seeming lack of attention. In the same way, I know I am unaware of how many times I fell short with my own children. We must all be aware that we will never be perfect. Even the most godly, caring parents miss it at times. We just do our best and pray for God to fill in the gaps. We must also look back with eyes of grace to when our parents (and others) missed it and extend the same forgiveness to them that we want for our own failings.

Antidote for Fear

Fear is bondage, and ultimately, we must see it for what it is and release it into God's hands. When we become a child of God and are adopted into His kingdom, we no longer need to live in fear. "For ye have not received the spirit of bondage again to fear; but ye have received the Spirit of adoption, whereby we cry, Abba, Father" (Romans 8:15).

God is love, and He calls us to love each other. "Beloved, let us love one another: for love is of God; and every one that loveth is born of God, and knoweth God" (1 John 4:7). John then says in verse 18, "There is no fear in love; but perfect love casteth out fear: because fear hath torment. He that feareth is not made perfect in love."

There is only one place to go with the fears that paralyze us and keep us in bondage. That is to our loving Father, the One whom we can trust to carry us through anything.

Writing Out Your Thoughts...

1. If you could go back to being a child, what are some worries, questions, or fears you would like to share? List them all, no matter how silly or small they seem to you now.

2. Did your fears ever make you feel so ashamed that they kept you from talking to someone? What is the worst thing you can imagine happening if you had told someone?

3. Did you ever hear something in church that caused a lot of fear? What was it?

4. What fears do you still have of God or specific Bible verses?

> *I sought the Lord, and he heard me, and delivered me from all my fears.* Psalm 34:4

Chapter 3

Learning to Cope

He was just my age. But he died?

My heart was in turmoil. *They said he fell down a hay hole and hurt his head. Then he went to be with Jesus.*

I knew the boy well, because he sat with his daddy in church and I sat with mine. He usually sat right in front of me, and I sometimes tried to put my shoe on his fingers when he wrapped them around the back of the bench. I knew it wasn't nice, but I did it anyway.

I wasn't nice to him. And now he died.

Many people were crying, including my mom and my siblings. I cried too, because my heart really hurt and I felt terrible. *Is God angry at me because I pinched his fingers against the bench?*

Inside me was a very confused, guilty feeling. Over and over, I asked God not to be angry with me and to forgive me. I cried and cried.

Sadness filled my heart. I looked at the sky when I went outside and wondered where the boy was. I thought about his mom and how she must miss him. *She must be so sad.* This made me cry even harder.

The world seemed scary. *Little people can die...* I felt so afraid.

Sitting between my two grandmothers, I felt tears streaming down my face. I couldn't stop. I looked for my mom, but I couldn't see either her or my dad. The ladies on the benches in front of me blocked my view.

I was afraid and unsettled, but I didn't know why. The tears just kept coming. One grandma handed me her fan and showed me how to open and close it. It was really pretty, but I kept crying and sniffling—loud enough that the ladies in front of us glanced back. My other grandma handed me a hanky with beautiful flowers, but I couldn't stop the tears. *Why can't I stop crying?*

I didn't know why I was crying. I just knew this church service was a big deal. When my daddy's name had been announced in church three days earlier, I saw my strong daddy get out his hanky and wipe his eyes. Later we got a lot of company, and even though I had fun, my stomach had an oily feeling. Something wasn't right. My siblings said Daddy could become a preacher, but I didn't know what that meant. I just knew people were sad—and sad made me cry.

Now as I sat in church and the minister preached on and on, I knew something wasn't right. *Why can't I sit with Mom or Dad?* My tears just wouldn't stop.

Finally my grandma told me to go out to the restroom, and my big sister followed me out. "What's wrong?" she asked. "Why are you crying?"

I didn't answer, because I didn't know. I just kept crying. I felt so nervous and afraid—and very, very sad.

I was seven years old.

I stood in the back row in our basement at school and ducked my head. As the melody of the song flowed through my ears and to my heart, I stopped singing to fight the tears. I knew fourth graders shouldn't cry (I was a big girl now), but I couldn't stop.

It happened almost every morning, and I didn't know why. The tune, the words... Somehow they got deep into my heart, and the tears would start. I tried to stop them but couldn't. When the other students looked my way, I ducked my head. I felt terrible shame. *Why am I crying?*

Songs about heaven and Jesus made me cry. I felt a stirring deep in my soul, and that seemed connected to my tears. I also thought of my mom and hoped she was okay. I loved my mom, and for some reason, singing made me think of her. As the tears flowed, I could hardly sing.

"Why do you cry when we sing?" one of the boys asked me at recess. He grinned, and I felt so ashamed. *I am weird. Why can't I be like the other children? They don't cry. Something must be wrong with me.*

I knew God had made me, so I wondered why He had made me like this. I prayed a lot, asking God to help me be tough, to help me not to cry.

But nothing changed. My heart remained sensitive, and many, many tears filled up my insides. Buckets of tears. They spilled over time and again, and I grew more and more ashamed. I learned to hide my tears.

I didn't talk about it and tried to act as if it didn't matter. But the hurt inside kept growing. Immature in my thinking and unable to process my emotions, I stuffed them down with many inner scoldings and shame.

Other girls don't cry like this. They don't mess up like I do. They can sing and not choke on tears. I despised who I was.

This is the thinking that controlled me as I grew older. No matter what happened, I blamed it on who I was. *If only I would be different.*

Whenever difficulties arose—within my family, at school, or even while doing chores—I scolded and belittled myself as I stuffed down the tears.

Learning to Cope

I remember standing in front of a mirror, giving myself a talking to.

Sometimes the hurt was more than I could squash down and the tears more than I could contain. I would find a quiet corner and sob until some of the pressure was released. I always felt so ashamed. *Why do I cry so much?*

I also had many happy childhood moments, and I wonder why I allowed myself to be so distracted by my sensitivity and tears. Memories of swimming, picking tea, riding my bike, playing baseball with my siblings, catching fireflies, swinging, and helping on the family farm fill me with warmth and delight.

Why couldn't I accept myself for who I was? Why couldn't I simply focus on the good and not worry so much about the things I couldn't understand? Why were my thinking threads so tangled—so knotted in negativity and despondency? Was it my personality? My genetics? The influences in my life? I look back now and see that it was probably all three.

Whatever the reason, I stepped into my teens with a prevailing mindset: *I am not a nice person.* I was filled with a fierce determination to control my world. *I will make myself lovable and not allow myself to be hurt. No one will see my tears!* I felt compelled to change who I was.

> I desperately stepped into the role of control—not realizing that I was stepping into a role that belonged to God.

I didn't know that squashing all these emotions would develop into a world so all-consuming that it would ruin parts of my life. I was ripe for an addiction, but I didn't realize it and probably wouldn't have cared.

Only one thing mattered—to be someone people would like. *I am fun and silly and can make people laugh. I can work hard and get things done. I am tough.* Desperately I tried to make myself into who I thought I should be.

If I can act like this, no one will know who I really am. If there were tears or pain, I quickly hid them. I learned to switch them to anger or frustration.

I didn't do this consciously. But now, as I look back at my tangled thinking, I see that I took what I thought was "wrong" and tried my best to make it "right." I desperately stepped into the role of control—not realizing that I was stepping into a role that belonged to God.

As I learned to hide my tears, I found I needed a "safe place." At night, when I couldn't sleep, the tears would fall as I begged God to forgive me for my failures. I was sure He couldn't love someone like me. I was bad. In a little place in the haymow, tucked away in the barn where no one could see, I allowed the tears to flow, all the while scolding myself for not being better, nicer, and sweeter. As the pain became more intense and confusing, so did my desperation to make myself into someone else.

When I made a mistake, I almost couldn't get over it. Even the simplest little thing got me into a tizzy. If I messed up doing a chore or said something I shouldn't have, I felt like a complete failure. In between scolding and berating myself, I cried out to God to help me not be so sensitive, to not hurt so much, to never mess up again. I didn't realize that I should pray that God would help me accept myself. Or that a perfectionist personality like mine needs careful tempering.

Mental pain is an anguish that can lead to physical pain. Since physical pain feels better than mental pain, I began hurting myself on purpose to shift the pain from mental to physical. Bruises or wounds on the outside felt better than the dark spots on the inside.

If only I had known what I know today—that pain shared is half the pain. But sadly, I had not yet learned to trust anyone with my deepest feelings.

If only I had shared...

Mentor's Thoughts

I have been fascinated by bloodhounds ever since I saw a demonstration of how one of these dogs unerringly tracked a young boy using only the scent from a stocking. I have since learned that bloodhounds have 300 million scent receptors in their nose, while humans have only 25 million. These dogs are important in tracking and finding things—anything from lost humans to illegal drugs.

Other dogs, such as Labrador retrievers and German shepherds, have incredibly sensitive hearing because of the creative design of their ears. They are of value to the hearing impaired or in protecting your home from a burglar.

These are just two examples of God's incredible creation. He created each of these dogs in a special way to be an asset to His world. With an owner who understands their unique talents, these dogs can perform a valuable service.

Just like these dogs, we are all born with differing degrees of sensitivity. Our central nervous system is where our five senses send information to be processed and responded to. But not everyone experiences sensory information in the same way. This is why one person barely smells something, but the next person is nauseated by the same smell. Some people just have a more finely tuned nervous system than others. It is the way God created them. Having a highly sensitive temperament is not a disorder; it is a God-given personality trait.

God created people with many unique talents and personalities, and each one is special and valuable in His kingdom. Highly sensitive people are perhaps the most misunderstood of all personality groups. These intuitive, thoughtful, compassionate, empathetic, conscientious, loyal, and creative individuals make up 15-20 percent of the population.

Many times, these uniquely gifted members of our society are the artists, writers, and singers. The often highly sensitive nature of these people allows them to find beauty and joy in things that others may not.

A highly sensitive person's brain works differently from that of the average person, with greater sensitivity to physical, emotional, spiritual, or social stimuli. Because of this, there is a greater reaction to both positive and negative influences. This means a highly sensitive person will have higher highs and lower lows.

Highly sensitive people are thus more affected by any kind of trauma. We usually think of trauma as a devastating event, and it normally is. For the highly sensitive child, however, trauma can come from something that doesn't appear to be all that devastating. A relatively small incident can flood the nervous system with overwhelming feelings of fear or shame.

> Having a highly sensitive temperament is not a disorder; it is a God-given personality trait.

That's why a funeral, an ordination, or a story or song can overwhelm a heart—not only by what is understood but also by the emotions of others. A harsh tone or negative response from someone can create devastating fear. So can a thunderstorm. The reason for the fear may not be clear, but the negativity is felt, and fear takes control. Being overwhelmed with these confusing or traumatic situations can cause an eating disorder as it did for Sarah, or it can lead to other disorders such as OCD (obsessive-compulsive

Learning to Cope

disorder), anxiety, depression, panic attacks, nightmares, and more.

In some cases, medication can help a person deal with an over-stimulated nervous system, and nutritional supplements or diet changes may also be helpful. It is important to learn what triggers the stress and then try to avoid those things or find healthy ways to cope with them. It is helpful to have a safe, quiet place to go to during times of stress.

For parents, the most powerful way to help a highly sensitive child is to be understanding. It will take extra time to listen and get to the root of the problem. Sometimes parents just need to hold the child patiently until the fear subsides. These children need to be affirmed and never shamed. It is okay to tell them there is nothing to be afraid of, but it must be done in a gentle way. Parents should try to affirm that it is all right to feel afraid or ashamed before quietly talking them through the fear or shame.

These children need lots of hugs and safe touch, but because they experience stimuli in a stronger way, parents must be very careful with negative touch. Pinching or slapping will affect them more intensely than a child with a less sensitive nervous system.

Parents should take time to teach their children about God as a loving Father who is always faithful. They should stress the truth that He loves them just as they are and not for what they do. Highly sensitive children have a tender conscience and will take to heart what they hear in church. If they hear a strong, adult-level sermon of sins condemning you to hell, they may translate that to mean they are doomed because they pulled the dog's tail.

If you are a highly sensitive adult, this may open your eyes to a new understanding of why you have always seemed to feel things more deeply than others. You may have felt like you were strange and unlovable—and maybe you still feel that way.

It is important to understand that you have been created with a greater sensitivity for a special purpose. What you do with that is your choice. You can choose to seek the Father's purpose for you, or you can be easily hurt and use your sensitivity in a way that requires everyone to tiptoe around you. This is using your sensitivity to manipulate others.

As your Creator, God is calling you to walk with Him. He wants you to seek His will and to understand who you are in Him. You have been uniquely created by God for a special purpose. To learn what that purpose is, you must learn to know the Father.

He invites us all to a closer walk with Him. Here are some verses to memorize and make a part of your life:

- For God so loved the world, that he gave his only begotten Son, that whosoever believeth in him should not perish, but have everlasting life. For God sent not his Son into the world to condemn the world; but that the world through him might be saved (John 3:16-17).

- Peace I leave with you, my peace I give unto you: not as the world giveth, give I unto you. Let not your heart be troubled, neither let it be afraid (John 14:27).

- These things have I spoken unto you, that in me ye might have peace. In the world ye shall have tribulation: but be of good cheer; I have overcome the world (John 16:33).

Writing Out Your Thoughts...

1. What are things about yourself that you are sure others cannot like?

2. Do you ever hurt yourself to express your pain inside? Does it help? Which lasts longer—the relief or the shame?

3. What makes you cry because of sadness? What beautiful things make you cry because they cause an ache in your heart?

4. Name something about yourself that you are sure God does not like.

> *Thou wilt keep him in perfect peace, whose mind is stayed on thee: because he trusteth in thee.* Isaiah 26:3

Part Two

Out of Control

Satan deceives us by letting us think we are in control, when in reality, we are not. The things we believe we need to do to be safe end up controlling us, becoming a painful bondage. This bondage, especially when combined with the nutritional depletion of an eating disorder, causes much confusion.

In Part Two, we see Sarah desperately trying to keep her fears at bay. She knows what she is doing is wrong, but she feels helpless to stop her actions.

chapter 4

No Pain—No Gain

It started subtly, but it wasn't long until it became normal for me—a focus on food. Continuous thoughts about food and eating marched through my mind. I was constantly aware of it.

Thoughts that I had a poochy belly, chubby legs, and big arms—though largely untrue—would hit me with such revulsion that I would vow anew to get my body under control. I would determine not to eat much, but when a meal came, it seemed I couldn't stop. I would eat and eat. Then it would hit me.

Shame. Deep, wrenching shame.

Shame filled me until it turned into a festering sore inside. I hated myself for not being "little and skinny" like I wanted to be. In my last years at school, I was throwing food from my lunch into the trash and hiding it. But at home, I often sneaked food and went somewhere private to eat it. I can't tell you why. It just became who I was.

I hated myself for it, but purging after a meal to rid myself of food became my normal routine. I also jumped rope to burn up calories and constantly checked myself in the mirror to see how fat I was. An angry chorus of self-deprecating thoughts were my constant companions. As the emotional turmoil became too heavy for me to comprehend, I became fixated on the outward.

This fixation was not only on my own physical appearance but also on those around me. Sure that others viewed me negatively, I learned to read their body movements and expressions. I became incredibly astute at watching people's reactions to gauge what they thought about me. I could quickly recognize when the teacher avoided eye contact or my chums' eyes darkened.

> I was also convinced that God would not accept me until I became who I thought I must be. It's called perfectionism, and it's a dangerous walk.

I knew immediately when I wasn't appreciated or was in trouble for something. I learned to read people so well that I could quickly discern when it was safe to laugh and joke and when people wanted me to be more serious.

Every time I walked into a room, I was awkwardly aware of my body and my movements, as well as the positions of those around me. I wanted to hide, but at the same time I craved attention. I wanted to be seen, to be loved, but I hated being in the spotlight. The constant tug and pull of these rogue feelings caused a lot of frustration inside.

For lack of a better way to describe it, I became obsessive about myself in a negative way. I didn't like my teary, sensitive self. I didn't like my body or how I walked or talked or acted. I didn't like my face, my smile, or that I needed glasses and braces. And I decided that most others felt the same way about me.

My number one goal was to make myself someone others would love and accept—and then maybe I could do the same. I was also convinced that God would not accept me until I became who I thought I must be.

It's called perfectionism, and it's a dangerous walk.

I didn't realize what treacherous ground I was treading on. Oh, I prayed. I prayed my little heart out, but they were always fear-filled, shameful prayers: "God, I'm sorry. I want to be nicer. Please help me be sweeter. To not make mistakes. Please help me to stop being so sensitive. Help me be brave. Make me a better person…"

Did God hear me? At one time in my life, I may have told you I'm not sure. But now I know without a doubt—absolutely! God heard every one of my confused prayers, and He knew what was best. He may not have given me what I asked for, but thankfully, He didn't leave me there.

As I entered my teen years with a distorted self-image, I learned of other ways to keep myself in control. Without hesitation, I followed some of my coworkers' examples and added the misuse of pills to my obsession to bring down my weight.

I became so obsessed with my weight that I became less concerned about pushing myself too far. Being accepted was everything! I was no longer innocently stumbling into an eating disorder—I was making specific choices that I knew could hurt me.

I found myself able to shut down my pain. If something hurt, I simply turned it off. This included both emotional pain and physical pain. I could go for a long time without eating and not even feel hungry. I could take way more pills than recommended. Because of this, I convinced myself that I was tough—and for a time, I was.

As people began to notice and make comments about my weight, it made me feel good. Powerful. I was finally making myself who I thought I should be.

The scale became my enemy. It was never right—the number never low enough. Every time I stepped on it, I felt the need to punish myself. As my trips to the scale became more and more frequent, the scale became a monster—my master.

My relationships with others were what I made them, but I didn't want anyone too close; I had too many secrets. People might learn about all the things I did.

Have you ever heard the quote about someone being "alone in a room full of people"? That was where I placed myself—by my own choice.

I knew how to act the part. By forcing myself to laugh, to be silly, to be the life of the party, I created the impression that I was confident, carefree, and sweet.

I became who I thought I should be. I was finally someone I could like. And someone others could like.

But I didn't realize how quickly this person I had worked so hard to create would make me miserable.

Mentor's Thoughts

One common trait of many disorders and mental imbalances is perfectionism. It takes over a mind that is desperately trying to find acceptance with self and others. Perfectionism causes people to be hypercritical of themselves and to have low self-esteem.

Striving for excellence is not wrong if done in a healthy way. Healthy perfectionism is the desire to do one's best but having a healthy view of oneself. It is being a high achiever but not basing one's worth on success. Unhealthy perfectionism, on the other hand, creates unrealistic demands and is never satisfied, causing much stress.

A drive for excellence is often a character trait—the personality you were born with. So how do you know if your desire to excel is healthy or not? How can you tell if a natural yearning for perfection has become unbalanced? Following are some ways it plays out:

Healthy perfectionism: A conscientiousness to do things well, with goal-directed behavior and good organizational skills. You set a high standard for yourself and others, but you are realistic. You do not base your worth on being the best, and you do not despair when you face adversity and things are not perfect.

Unhealthy perfectionism: A striving to be looked up to—to be the best at all costs. You become critical of yourself and others, with constant doubts that things are being done correctly. There is a need to be in control, with an excessive focus on past mistakes and the possibility of making new ones.[1]

As unhealthy perfectionism takes over your life and your thoughts, you become terrified of failing. You think you are never good enough, so you procrastinate, fearing failure. You stress out over little things and become uptight. You get defensive easily and struggle to share your thoughts and feelings. You become controlling in your relationships.

Unhealthy perfectionism often becomes an obsession. This is a preoccupation with a certain idea or feeling—often an unreasonable one. In Sarah's story, we can see the ways her obsessive thinking became unreasonable. Is it reasonable to think of food all the time—whether to avoid it or to get more of it? Is it reasonable to constantly evaluate ourselves in the mirror? Or to purge the food we eat?

Obsessive thinking leads to an unhealthy focus on self. This leads

---

[1] For more on perfectionism, see https://www.samhealth.org/about-samaritan/news-search/2021/05/10/is-perfectionism-healthy-tame-your-inner-taskmaster.

to a preoccupation with trying to protect ourselves and thus controlling what happens around us. We become super aware of what others think of us and how we appear to them. We were not created for this stress on our nervous system. If this is not dealt with, it will lead to further anxiety disorders.

How Can I Change?

It is possible to let go of unhealthy perfectionism and learn to be easier on yourself, but it takes conscious effort. You will need to become aware of what you are thinking.

> The only way to have a healthy view of ourselves is to understand how God the Father sees us.

One thing to watch for is "all-or-nothing" thinking. This kind of thinking sees everything in black and white—in absolutes. If you make a mistake, you think it's horrible. *I can never do anything right. I'm just going to quit trying.*

The first step in overcoming the tendency to think like this is to pay attention to what you are thinking. Ask yourself if your thoughts are actually true. It is helpful to write down the thoughts that drive you—the thoughts that say you must do this or that to be accepted or be okay. This will engage the logical part of your brain and help you discern what is truth and what is emotional thinking. When you analyze your thoughts in a purposeful way, you can learn to let them go if they are destructive.

It can be helpful to observe how others accept their imperfections. Everyone makes mistakes. How do they cope with them? It is very important to open up about your feelings, so find a person you can trust and tell him or her what you are struggling with.

Our fears about what people think of us are usually not grounded in truth, so we must be careful not to view people's actions and words as personal attacks. Most likely they are not. We must choose to forgive them—and to give them the benefit of the doubt.

For our own mistakes, we must tell ourselves that the way God made us is good enough. We should do our best, but then we must accept ourselves as we are.

The only way to have a healthy view of ourselves is to understand how God the Father sees us. As we learn to see ourselves through His eyes of love and acceptance, it becomes easier to accept ourselves as an imperfect creation made perfect through Jesus.

Following are some verses to memorize and make a part of your life:

- But ye are a chosen generation, a royal priesthood, an holy nation, a peculiar people; that ye should shew forth the praises of him who hath called you out of darkness into his marvellous light (1 Peter 2:9).

- And he said unto me, My grace is sufficient for thee: for my strength is made perfect in weakness (2 Corinthians 12:9).

- But even the very hairs of your head are all numbered. Fear not therefore: ye are of more value than many sparrows (Luke 12:7).

- Being confident of this very thing, that he which hath begun a good work in you will perform it until the day of Jesus Christ (Philippians 1:6).

Reality Check…Check each one that is a "yes."

☐ Do you feel in control of your life only when you control your food and weight?

☐ Do you feel terrible shame if you gain even a little weight?

☐ Do you feel you are worthy of love only when you are thin, look a certain way, or do everything perfectly?

☐ Do you compare yourself with other people's physical appearances?

☐ Do you consider yourself fat even when people around you comment on how thin you are? Or ugly even if you are told you are pretty?

Writing Out Your Thoughts…

1. Do you find it easier to focus on the outward things? What do you do to keep from having to look at the pain and ugliness inside you?

2. Do you think you must be perfect in everything you do? In what ways? Are there people in your life who make you feel you can never be good enough?

3. How is your obsessive thinking like Sarah's? What are things you obsess or worry about?

4. What parts of yourself do you not like? Are any of these changeable? How could you change them?

5. What things don't you like about yourself that are unchangeable (hair, teeth, nose, parents, place in the family, etc.)?

> I will praise thee; for I am fearfully and wonderfully made: marvellous are thy works; and that my soul knoweth right well. Psalm 139:14

To Ponder

Have you ever considered that your unchangeable parts are how God designed you? Although we cannot always know why, He has created you uniquely YOU for a very special reason. Look at what you do not like about yourself and then think about God's purpose for you. Could this be God's "mark of ownership" in your life?

Take this unchangeable to your Father and thank Him for His mark of ownership, then ask Him to help you to see it (and yourself) through His eyes.

chapter
5

The Lie

I shouldn't have taken so many pills... The thought sent a shock of fear through me.

Doubled over in violent stomach pain, my prayers took a frantic turn. "Please, God, help me. I promise I won't do it again...Please help me be okay. O God, I'm sorry."

My mind raced. This wasn't the first time I was in this position. Frightening as it was, I had been here time and again. My intestines constricted tightly; I couldn't breathe. As another wave of pain hit me, I tensed my body to ride it out. *Have I pushed it too far? What if I have done serious damage? What if...?* Suddenly I was scared.

Shame flooded my entire being. Deep, desperate shame. *I have to stop doing this.* Tears ran down my cheeks.

Though self-inflicted, the pain created a turmoil in my heart that I can't describe. On one hand, it was my own fault. After all, I'm the one who took the pills that caused my stomach and intestines to cramp in pain. On the other hand, it felt like the only choice I had.

The food had to go!

I didn't know at the time that there were others like me. I didn't even know that eating disorders exist. My battle was so deeply hidden, so personal, that I couldn't begin to explain the feelings and thoughts that surrounded it. I hated it, but I felt helpless to do anything about it.

> Satan's biggest lie in this tangled web is that we are alone—that there is no one to help.

I didn't know there were others fighting the same battle, though perhaps in different ways. I truly believed it was just me.

Steeped in shame, I knew there was no way I could share this awful fight. No one would understand the turmoil inside my mind.

The turmoil that kept me from eating—or to overeat and then purge. The turmoil that prompted me to take an excessive number of pills to rid my body of food. The turmoil that motivated me to exercise until my body trembled with exhaustion. I was sure no one would understand the horrible shame I experienced every time I did it.

No, I can't tell anyone. They would find out who I am.

I knew I was not taking care of my body, but my body seemed to be my enemy. I prayed, but I didn't think God would hear me. *He is likely angry with me,* I reasoned. I was sure no other woman—especially a Christian, God-fearing one—would ever do anything like this.

Eventually the stomach pain subsided, and the empty, washed-out feeling I was familiar with brought me comfort. Although I had frantically prayed for God to help me and made promises not to do it again, I shut down the earlier conviction with new thoughts: *It wasn't that bad. You can keep on. If you don't, you will be fat. Just be careful not to overdo it... You are okay now. See? It won't be as bad the next time.*

With that, I buried my desire for change and continued making the same choices, fighting the same thoughts, and choosing the only way that seemed acceptable.

I grew more and more deceptive, finding ways to hide my food consumption, my purging, my disordered thinking. I focused on making my outward facade more and more lovable, doing everything I could to please those around me by whatever means possible.

Doing this could eventually take my life, I knew, but somehow that didn't scare me very much. I felt like I was in control of what I was doing. *As long as no one knows, I am fine. There is nothing wrong with me. I'm okay as long as I'm careful.*

What an evil lie.

Satan's biggest lie in this tangled web is that we are alone—that there is no one to help, no way out, and we must be in control. He whispers so many things, mixing lies with God's Word and clouding our thinking so we can't see the truth. I was blessed to be born in a home where I learned God's Word, but the evil one twisted things just enough to confuse me. And then he caused me to believe I couldn't tell anyone.

It wasn't until years later that I realized I am not my own. I am under the care of the almighty God! I have learned that I am more in control when I give up control to Him—to the One who actually is in control. The One who loves me so much that He died for me. I am so thankful that I eventually learned this.

But it has been a lifelong process.

One of the most helpful things I have learned is to confide in others. When I face a struggle, I now share with others. I tell a friend...

And right now, sharing my awful bondage with readers who face brokenness of their own is the best way for me to put it to rest.

Mentor's Thoughts

Purging is one of the most devastating lies of eating disorders. This lie says that if I eat, I have to get rid of the food before it can make me fat. But what makes sense to a mind trapped in an eating disorder actually goes against science and the way our bodies have been created to function. Let's look at some of these deceptions.

- **The lie says, "If I am forced to eat, I can get rid of the food so I don't gain weight."**

    Satan is the master deceiver. You may think vomiting up what you ate is a good, safe way to get rid of what you wish you hadn't eaten. God's science says the opposite.

    Regularly purging your food in this way lowers your metabolism because it restricts the calories your body has to digest. This can lead to starvation mode, which is your body's natural response to a severe calorie deficit. This will cause your body to store up the few calories it gets and can actually hamper your ability to lose weight.

    Purging is also harmful in other ways. Vomiting up your food exposes your throat and mouth to stomach acid, which can damage the esophagus and lead to tooth decay and gum disease. Purging in any way causes dehydration, causing electrolyte and mineral imbalances. This can damage the heart and other organs.

    Most people who fall for these lies are unaware of all the physical harm purging can do. The sidebar on the next page gives additional information on the long-term effects of forced vomiting, laxatives, diet pills, diuretics, and excessive exercise.

Effects of Purging on the Body [1]

Heart and Other Organs: Frequent purging causes dehydration, throwing the electrolytes out of balance and straining the heart and other organs. People with bulimia are five times more likely to have a heart attack than those without an eating disorder. It can also cause an irregular heartbeat.

Prolonged dehydration can lead to urinary tract infections, kidney stones, and kidney failure, which can be fatal.

Teeth and Mouth: When you repeatedly vomit, you are risking serious damage to your teeth. The stomach acid in the vomit corrodes the enamel that protects your teeth, resulting in cavities, gingivitis (inflamed gums), and brittle and sensitive teeth.

Stomach acid can also cause swelling of the salivary glands around the jaw and cheeks and cause sores in the mouth and throat.

Hair: When the body does not get the nutrients it needs, it will take them from other sources, such as hair. Your hair may become dry and frizzy, or even fall out. As your body focuses on keeping you alive, hair growth may stop altogether.

Eyes: Pressure on the eyes from forced vomiting may cause them to become red and irritated. Blood vessels may break, causing large red patches in the white of the eye. Eye sockets often become sunken in, and dark circles appear under the eyes.

Skin: Dehydration causes the skin to become dry and scaly. The cheeks and other parts of the face may become swollen.

Reproductive System: Purging may cause hormonal imbalances and can sometimes stop female menstrual cycles.

Mood and Stress: Purging and other eating disorder actions are often the result of other emotional issues, including depression, anxiety, bipolar disorder, and post-traumatic stress disorder (PTSD). Purging then worsens these disorders, leading to feelings of guilt, irritability, secrecy, anxiety, and stress. It is a vicious cycle.

---

[1] For more on the effects of purging, see veritascollaborative.com/blog/how-does-purging-affect-the-body/.

- **The lie says, "If I take laxatives, the food will leave my body too quickly to make me fat."**

  If we understand the way laxatives work, we can see that this is another eating disorder lie. When we eat food, it enters our stomach first, where it is broken down by digestive juices. It then goes to the small intestine, where the carbohydrates, fats, proteins, vitamins, and minerals are absorbed into our body.

  It is only what is left, the waste and extra fluid, that enters the large intestine, which is what laxatives stimulate to empty. Since everything of value has already been absorbed, the only "weight" you are losing is waste and fluid.

  > Most people who fall for these lies are unaware of all the physical harm purging can do.

- **The lie says, "If I take diuretics, I can lose weight quickly."**

  Diuretics are drugs to help rid the body of excess fluid that could cause medical problems. People sometimes think taking diuretics is an easy way to get rid of extra weight.

  Though this may work to shed a little weight quickly, it is only temporary. Using diuretics long-term actually causes your body to retain more fluids, leading to bloating and weight gain. Side effects of diuretic abuse include dizziness, constipation, dehydration, low blood pressure, kidney damage, abnormal heart rate, potassium deficiency, and more.

- **The lie says, "If I just don't eat, or eat very little, I will lose weight and be as thin as I want to be."**

God's science—the way He created us—says that our bodies need to receive healthy nourishment at regular intervals to function properly. If we skip too many meals and reduce our calorie intake too much, our body will slow down its metabolism and go into starvation mode. This God-given mechanism helps the body maintain energy balance and prevents starvation. When your body does not know where its next nourishment is coming from, it will store up any nutrition it gets to help maintain energy balance until more nourishment is received.

One part of this lie says that if you cut fats completely out of your diet, you will be as thin as you need to be and still be okay. That is not true; your body needs healthy fats to function properly. The word *fat* makes us think of sweet, fattening foods that cause us to gain weight, but not all fats are like this. The main fats to avoid are the trans fats found in processed foods.

Healthy fats such as those found in nuts, seeds, olive oil, etc. are a needed part of our diet. These fats raise good cholesterol (HDL) and lower bad cholesterol (LDL), maintain brain health, fight inflammation, and more. The type of fat matters more than the calorie count. Good fats will also help us feel full and curb cravings. But as with all food, even good fats need to be consumed in moderation to be healthy.

If your body does not receive enough nutrition to stay healthy, you will eventually reach that dangerous place where starvation starts to set in. At that point, your body will take drastic measures to protect itself with symptoms like lanugo, a fine, downy hair growth on certain parts of your body, often the back and shoulders.[1] Trying to pull your body back from the brink of this death walk takes time. During this time, it is very important to follow a regular schedule of eating a balanced diet until your metabolism heals and your health is restored.

- **The lie says, "If I exercise enough after eating, I can rid my body of the calories before they turn to fat."**

Exercise is good for you and most of us could use more. However, it can become an addiction and an obsession. Thirty minutes a day of moderate physical activity is enough to prevent health issues like diabetes, high cholesterol, and high blood pressure. But it becomes obsessive when you think a two-hour run will make you four times healthier. It just doesn't work that way.

Too much exercise has a negative impact on your body and will produce results that are the exact opposite of what you want. Exhaustion, depression, hormonal imbalance, skewed metabolism, and more can result from over-exercise. Healthy exercise is when you organize your exercise time around your life, not the other way around.

Physical activity can be a positive way to deal with anxiety. But when done in excess, it becomes a slave driver and puts you in bondage. Instead of exercise being something good, it becomes a punishment for eating.

---

[1] It is believed that lanugo grows to help insulate a body that is not receiving enough nutrition to regulate its own temperature. The presence of this soft, feathery hair is a sign that it's high time to get medical help. For more on this, see https://www.webmd.com/mental-health/eating-disorders/what-to-know-lanugo-and-anorexia.

Listening to these lies brings devastating consequences. Not only will it cause physical havoc to your body, but there are also the spiritual ramifications of giving in to these lies. It will distract you from God's purpose for your life and will distort your relationship with Him—and with other people. It will bring you into a bondage you do not want.

When you face these devastating lies, recognize them for what they are—lies.

Reality Check...Check each one that is true.

- ☐ Do you believe purging will keep you from gaining weight and make you thin?
- ☐ Do you take actions to keep yourself thin at all costs?
- ☐ Do you believe the best way to be thin is to avoid all food?
- ☐ Do you believe there are foods that are "good" or "bad"?
- ☐ Do you often feel afraid and ashamed of your eating behaviors?
- ☐ Do you feel a sense of power when you use these methods to control your food intake?
- ☐ Do you ever feel an irresistible urge to exercise more and more?

Writing Out Your Thoughts...

1. What foods do you consider unsafe to eat? What rules do you follow in choosing what is okay to eat?

2. How does it make you feel to learn that the methods you have been using to avoid weight gain could actually be causing you to store fat? Do you believe what science is telling you?

3. Do you ever want to eat but feel you don't deserve food? What events or reasons might trigger these feelings?

4. Have you believed the lies mentioned in this chapter? Which ones? Can you accept that they are not true?

> *Be not deceived; God is not mocked: for whatsoever a man soweth, that shall he also reap.* Galatians 6:7

chapter
6

One Girl—Two Lives

Every day we make many choices, some of them potentially life-changing. Every day we choose life or death.

Deuteronomy 30:19 is a verse I have chosen as my own: "I call heaven and earth to record this day against you, that I have set before you life and death, blessing and cursing: therefore choose life, that both thou and thy seed may live."

Although these words were spoken by Moses to the children of Israel when God was giving them direction, I have felt God calling me to the same account many times.

When we are caught in bondage, our freedom of choice seems to be taken from us. Instead of understanding that we have the power to make life-changing choices, our vision becomes narrow, and we make desperate minute-by-minute choices. We don't consider the results of our choices, whether they are for life or for death. Instead, we make our choices out of our bondage—and that will always bind us tighter.

With a mind clouded and bound by an eating disorder, every situation I faced made me cling more desperately to that one area in my life I could control: I could choose what I put in my mouth. If someone forced me to eat, or if I had to eat to appear normal, I would. But no one could make me keep it. No one could control what I did with my own body. I had a tight grip on things.

I cannot say that these were distinct thoughts or purposeful choices. And that's the dangerous part. It wasn't something I planned or thought out, I just fell into it, slowly but surely. It became a way of life, like taking a shower or washing the floor.

Like all types of bondage, it simply took over.

But at the same time, I was deeply sensitive to God and wanted to please Him. I would cry out to Him one moment and make bad choices the next. I became two different people.

On the one hand, I was finding my own way through life's pain and circumstances, trusting in all the ways the eating disorder helped me cope. I was tough, confident, and outgoing, but also secretive.

On the other hand, I pleaded to God in brokenness, asking for His help and forgiveness. I continually felt bad and unworthy, but I also lived in fear of God, wanting desperately to be good enough to make Him love me. I was horrified of hell and afraid of God, because I believed He could send me there. Knowing my unworthiness, I feared there was no way He would allow me into heaven.

I truly accepted Jesus as my Savior and was baptized. I gave my life to Him, and with all my heart I meant to be a different person. For a few weeks I stopped some of my eating disorder tendencies, but all too soon I fell back into them. But no one knew...

My relationships at work became a detriment to me. It was like another world. The friends I had there were nothing like my church friends. But I knew how to be friends with both. I could be who I needed to be, whether at home, at work, or at church. I became increasingly confused about who I really was.

It was time to make a choice. I could not continue to flip-flop between two opposing paths.

Everyone born into this fallen world of sin will face pain and trauma at some point. It is inevitable. The question is how we handle it. Where do we go with our pain? What do we do with it?

Everyone's experience is different. Your story is uniquely yours, and you will need to face, head-on, whatever pain and trauma life brings. How should you face it? First of all, hand in hand with Jesus and with the Word of God in your heart.

> In one way or another, pain that is not dealt with will fester and manifest itself.

And second, never face it alone. Share your pain. If there is anything I can shout out as a flag of warning to Satan's tactics, it is that he will try to silence you. He will try to convince you that you are utterly alone, that no one will understand, that you will be considered weird or crazy if you tell anyone. But don't believe it. No matter what you have done, or what you have seen or faced, you are not alone.

If anyone tells you otherwise, don't listen, because it is a lie! Even when bad things happen, we are not alone.

Though no one else was around when I was shoved up against the wall in the back aisle of my workplace and fondled by a man three times my age, his hot beer breath in my face, I wasn't alone. I managed to get away and back to the safety of my coworkers, frightened and shaking. Then I did what I had done from a little girl on up—I didn't say a word. But even though I kept it a complete secret for many years, feeling yucky and used, I wasn't alone.

I wasn't alone when a tragic accident claimed the life of one of my favorite coworkers. The same one who had asked me about my faith in God and to whom I had given a flippant answer... As I faced the horrifying realization that I had missed my chance to share Jesus with her, I felt completely alone. But instead of sharing my grief with others, I tucked it deep down inside, not sure how to face it.

When a two-year relationship with a nice Christian young man ended, by my choice, I wasn't as alone as I believed. Or when the next relationship also failed. Nor was I alone when I realized that a woman I considered a friend at work was actually a predator looking for more than friendship in a way of which I was completely innocent.

For all these hurts, I reacted the same way. I tucked them deep down inside where I was sure I wouldn't have to think about them, and they would disappear forever. But that's not what happened. That pile of hurts kept oozing and festering, growing bigger and more unstable with each added painful experience. Each one reinforced my view of myself as a low-down, worthless mistake—one who could never do anything right.

You have your own story, and you will face your own trauma and pain. But don't make the same mistake I did. Don't think you can bury it and it will disappear. It won't; it will come out. It may take years, but in some way it will come out.

Often it manifests itself as anger. Other times it can come out as gossip, where we point out others' faults in an effort to make ourselves look better. We become cynical and sarcastic, looking good on the outside but feeling hopelessly lost on the inside. We might be the joker in the group, but inwardly feel very alone.

Sometimes hidden pain manifests itself by feeling the need to be in charge. When challenged, we get annoyed or lash out in frustration and anger. In one way or another, pain that is not dealt with will fester and manifest itself. It will eventually come out.

Mine came out in an eating disorder.

Pills, purging, hiding, and lying became a big part of my life. I honestly believed it was "just me." No big deal. *I am fine.* Oh, I knew I couldn't tell anyone, but it wasn't a big deal.

But that only lasts so long.

When I was nineteen years old, I again committed my life to God in a friend's basement. It seemed I could never hold on to peace, so I continually asked God into my heart. This time, though, I was determined to do better. But like so often before, I was successful for only a few weeks before I slowly but surely fell back into the same things. Always secretive. Always hiding things. And even more ashamed.

Despite my secret life, I made a few close friendships during my teen years. I loved these friends dearly and found a lot of joy and peace when I could be with them. Since they went to the same church conference, their friendships built me up in many good ways. I don't recall sharing much of my struggle with them, but I did share a lot of personal things. I wonder what choices I would have made if it hadn't been for these friends. Again, God looked out for me in a way I didn't realize until years later.

> No one who hides so much can have a close relationship.

Going on twenty years old, I tried to be on top of everything. And I could do it; nothing bothered me. I was the life of the party—silly and ready for anything. I was smart and witty and had lots of friends. I was full of energy and didn't need much sleep or rest. That was the surface me. The me I tried hard to maintain. The me people seemed to like.

Only a few persistent friends saw into the part of me that cried myself to sleep at night and struggled to stay on top of depression and discouragement. These friends knew I wasn't very stable. They saw my sleeplessness, my trips to the bathroom after eating, and my confusion about who I was and what salvation really meant. These friends heard my tears in our phone calls—when I allowed myself to open up a bit. They and my family must have been alarmed as they put up with my "strange" ways.

In a mercy I didn't recognize for many years, God brought a man into my life who simply accepted me as I was. He had integrity and a steadiness that God knew I needed. Our courtship was sometimes rocky, but he loved me enough to put up with some of what I now see as unreasonable demands and viewpoints. He was truly a God-send in my life. Through my incredible emotional ups and downs, he stayed with me and tried to understand me. But I didn't share everything with him either.

As I prepared for our wedding day, I focused mainly on outward preparation. I didn't want to look inside; it was too painful—the hatred for myself, the feelings of unworthiness and ugliness, the deep shame, the fear. Instead, I focused on losing weight for the wedding; that was something I could control. *After I am married,* I thought, *surely things will go better.* But I never really looked very far ahead. I couldn't.

On a very warm day in June, we were married. Although excited, I was nervous and unsure—but I truly loved my new husband. He had already proved that he was faithful. I had tested him in every way I could think of, and he had remained right there. He was steady and solid, and I accepted his place in my life. He was my husband, and I loved him as much as I could at the time.

But no one who hides so much can have a close relationship. The wounds I had hidden were festering...

Within a few short months, the changes in my life forced me to spin out of control, and I found myself at a crossroads. I could play the game no longer.

I needed to be one girl—God's girl—leading one life. Not two.

Mentor's Thoughts

Disorders, depression, and other problems can often be traced to the root of not understanding who God is or what salvation really means. Fear then grows from this misunderstanding.

What does it mean to be a child of God? What do I need to do?

How can I be good enough for a perfect God? What if I mess up? Sometimes we make it so complicated that our children get confused, and that confusion can follow into adulthood. What does God's Word say?

Paul explains it very simply in Romans 10:9: "That if thou shalt confess with thy mouth the Lord Jesus, and shalt believe in thine heart that God hath raised him from the dead, thou shalt be saved."

Is it really that simple? Jesus said similar words in John 5:24: "Verily, verily, I say unto you, He that heareth my word, and believeth on him that sent me, hath everlasting life, and shall not come into condemnation; but is passed from death unto life."

It is that simple. If you confess (or acknowledge) that you believe in your heart that Jesus is the Son of God who died and rose again to pay for your sins, you allow Him to become Lord of your life. That is all you need to do to become a child of God. You are passed from death to life; you are no longer under condemnation.

Romans 8:1 says, "There is therefore now no condemnation to them which are in Christ Jesus, who walk not after the flesh, but after the Spirit." Are you in Christ Jesus? According to what Jesus said, if you hear the Word and believe on God, then you are a Christian.

One of the most devastating lies Satan would have us believe is that God only loves us when we are good. Romans 5:8 tells us a simple truth: "But God commendeth his love toward us, in that, while we were yet sinners, Christ died for us." We do not have to be "good" first and then God accepts us. He calls us to come just as we are because of His great love for us.

Suppose you have been driving on muddy roads and your car is covered with mud. You need to take it to the carwash because it needs cleaning. The question is, do you need to wash the car before taking it to the carwash? Of course not. That's what a carwash is for—to clean the car. That is what happens when we come to Jesus and ask Him to cleanse us. He takes our past sins and removes the guilt of them. "I will remember their sin no more" (Jeremiah 31:34).

Will the car get dirty again? Yes. Will we still fail at times? Most certainly. But now, as a child of God, we bring our "dirt"—our failings and goof-ups—to Him and say we are sorry. 1 John 1:9 says, "If we confess our sins, he is faithful and just to forgive us our sins, and to cleanse us from all unrighteousness." As Jesus told the woman in John 8, He still tells us today, "Neither do I condemn thee: go, and sin no more."

I have heard salvation described as inviting Jesus into our heart-house. After we invite Him in, He steps into the entryway and we are His. But the rest of our "house" still needs His cleansing touch. As we walk with Jesus and learn more about Him through God's Word, He will point out more and more "rooms" that need to be cleaned.

> As we walk with Jesus and learn more about Him through God's Word, He will point out more and more "rooms" that need to be cleaned.

When God points out an area that needs to be cleaned, it is not because He is harsh; it is because He loves us. He knows that anything we hold dearer than Him will hurt us. He does not condemn us but lovingly shows how to live a life of freedom in Him.

Living in freedom means walking with the Lord and making good choices every day. It means living in openness to our Father, who loves us and cares for us—and who daily continues to work on our weak areas to make us more like Him. It is a process that is never done.

Walking with the Lord is a lifelong journey.

Writing Out Your Thoughts...

1. Do you ever feel like a different person depending on who you are with or where you are? Explain.

2. What trauma has shaped your life? Are there things in the past that scared you or made you sad, but you never shared with anyone?

3. Do you feel alone? Is there at least one person in your life with whom you feel safe to share anything?

4. What feels out of control in your life? What areas do you feel you can control?

5. Do you believe and confess that Jesus died and rose from the dead? Have you asked Him to come in and take over your life?

6. Do you feel like you need to try harder to be good? Do you have things hidden inside that you are sure God could never forgive?

Casting all your care upon him; for he careth for you. 1 Peter 5:7

To Ponder

Is the Gospel just a story to you? Have you heard the words, but you never really understood them or took them deeply into your own heart? Do you believe in God but not really know Him as your Father?

God is calling and knocking for you to allow Him deeper into your heart-house. He has so much more for you.

chapter 7

Dragged Back From the Cliff

Racing around on the blacktop at the daycare where I now worked, I bounced the basketball and made the shot. *Swish!* Perfect. The children cheered as I grinned in triumph. Then suddenly my world began to spin.

I ducked my head and staggered slightly. My heart pounded violently. One of the teacher's aides came to my side. "Are you okay?" she asked, grabbing my arm.

I sat down on the grass as the children gathered around me. Slowly my world came back into focus.

"I'm fine," I said, my always-ready answer. "I just need a drink of water."

Feeling weak was becoming a pretty normal occurrence for me. Deep inside I knew why, but I wouldn't look at it. *When did I last eat properly? A Mountain Dew yesterday afternoon?* I wasn't sure, and I really didn't care. But right now I needed something. I had learned by trial and error how far I could push myself and still be okay. Lately, however, it seemed I couldn't keep things under control.

I felt anger rising inside me. *I'm such a loser! I can't even go two days without food!* The barrage of negative thinking that normally kept me tightly controlled now made me afraid. Ever since I had gotten married, my life seemed to spin just a little off course.

> When we stuff all the bad emotions, we also limit the good ones.

I had been so excited to start a new life with my husband. I knew married life would be different, but the changes had rocked my world more than I had anticipated. It was now spinning beyond what I could control. It seemed the worst part of me was taking over. I was living on pills and soda and just enough food to stay upright. If I really needed to eat, I did my best to make sure my body didn't keep it for long.

My dear husband was so kind, but he knew this wasn't okay. With both of us working, I had more freedom and less accountability than I had at home. This made it easier for me to escape with no food.

My husband wanted to be close to me, but I was too afraid. I didn't know how to really love—because when we stuff all the bad emotions, we also limit the good ones. I had trouble feeling any emotion. More often than not, I pushed my husband away because I didn't want to hurt him the way I was hurting myself.

It wasn't that people didn't try to help me. Some expressed their concern, but my answer was always the same: "I'm okay." As long as I wasn't willing to accept help, there was little anyone could do.

I had to be smacked in the face with reality.

Some people with less determination may be quicker to reach for help and admit failure, but for me that has never been easy. I have been given an inner determination and a lot of competitiveness, sometimes downright stubbornness, which I had learned to mask under a happy-go-lucky exterior.

If I can give some gentle advice to anyone caught in any kind of bondage, it is to be humble enough to ask for help. If we aren't willing to do that, God will allow us to hit the very bottom. And that, my friends, is not an easy place to be.

As my life continued to spiral downward, I shed many tears. I can't describe the pain I dealt with. And honestly, by now I had no idea how to handle it. I began turning my inner emotional pain and spiritual turmoil into physical pain that I could handle.

After a "session" of purposeful self-harm, I would shake and weep. It left my arms and legs bruised and my heart confused—and all of me absolutely ashamed. It also brought another dimension of secrecy. Now I needed to make sure all my bruises were hidden under layers of clothing.

I was sick—emotionally, physically, and spiritually—but I didn't know how to fix it. My need for perfection and control was now beyond what I could handle. I knew I was ruining my life, but I didn't know what to do about it. When my husband and my friends encouraged me to get help, it just irritated me, and the battle became worse.

I couldn't sleep without sleeping pills, and then I couldn't get going without a pick-me-up. I had to eat for energy, but then I hated myself for eating. It became a vicious cycle that wore me out.

Sometimes God sends roadblocks to stop us from our destructive course. These may feel painful at the time, but when we look back, we can see His hand was there to protect us.

God used my employer and friend at the daycare where I worked to force my hand. She called me into her office one day and sat me down. She had been watching me with growing concern. In a conversation that had me in tears, she made me write down what I had eaten in the last four days and how many pills I had taken. She also questioned me very bluntly about my bruises and dizzy spells. For the first time, I was forced to look realistically at the destructive course I was on.

"You have an eating disorder," she told me kindly, but in a no-nonsense tone. "Many women battle this—you are not alone." I shook my head, but

Dragged Back From the Cliff

she put her hand on mine and held it in both of hers. "Yes, you do." Her voice was kind but firm.

I hung my head in shame, but I felt no condemnation from her. She cried with me, but she didn't stop there. She handed me a paper with a name on it. "Call this woman," she said. "She is a Christian counselor—a very nice woman. You are sick, and you must get help. You have to do it soon."

Seeing me shrink back from the idea, she said some of the hardest words for me to hear: "If you don't go, I can't let you work here. What if something happens when you are in charge of the children? I can't trust you with them."

She had hit me where it hurt deeply. I loved children. I always have. And I loved my job. I was pouring my heart into these little people.

But there was also a ray of hope. For the first time, I felt a lifeline being offered to rescue me from myself. She had named my problem and said I wasn't alone. She understood. Maybe...just maybe...I could live differently.

In heartrending sobs, I finally agreed to make the call. But I was so secretive. I didn't want people to know anything about my getting help. Only my husband.

My employer stayed right with me through it all. I made that first call and began talking to Mary. We did phone calls for a month or so before I agreed to come to her office.

My first trip to Mary's office was with my employer. When I got into her car, she laid a red rose on the dash. "It will stay there as a reminder for me to pray for you," she said, her voice shaking. The rose blurred in my vision as I felt her love. I had no idea what the future held, but that rose symbolized an intervention to save my life. It was still there, dried but beautiful, when I eventually quit my job at the daycare two years later.

The next few months were difficult. Although I was going for help, I still wasn't at the end of my rope. I knew what to say and when to say it—and what to do and what not to do. I had become a master of deception, and that mindset doesn't break easily. I told my counselor what I wanted her to know and no more.

But she wasn't buying it.

The visits to her were like a game of push and pull. Mary would push and I would pull away. She would talk and talk, and I would relax enough to say a little, but then I would clam up and yank my heart and my feelings back inside. She wanted me to admit that I needed help, but my quiet stubbornness wouldn't let me. Jaw set, I slammed the door shut on my heart and my emotions. I didn't want to like her. I didn't want to trust her or let her inside my head and heart.

I remember with humiliation a pat down as Mary showed me how bony my body really was. She pointed out my arms, my legs, my ribs, by running her hands over them and describing them. I detested it, but her point was made—I could no longer tell her I was fat. The knowledge that she was right only made me more frustrated. I *liked* to be this way; I *needed* to be this way. She was the one who didn't understand.

Finally, at one office visit, Mary pulled up a list of inpatient treatment centers on her computer and asked me to sit beside her while we looked at them. I was horrified. No way was I going to stay somewhere to get help. *If I do that, everyone will know.* I started shaking. This wasn't my game anymore.

Mary may have done it on purpose, because now I was listening. She made me look her in the eye. "Okay," she said, "I know you don't want to go anywhere, but I need help." In a rare display of emotion, she got teary-eyed, getting my attention.

"Listen to me, Sarah," she said, "we are not getting anywhere. You are getting worse, not better, and I need more help and advice. I love you too much to just let you fade away. God won't let me."

During that visit, she laid out my options. And there weren't many. In order to keep seeing her, I had to agree to see a doctor and get a physical. Otherwise, she was not comfortable in continuing, and we would need to look at more intense therapy.

I was caught. I couldn't stop with the counseling, or I would lose my job. And to continue to see my counselor, I had to do what she said.

Dragged Back From the Cliff

..rt. The pressure built up inside as I fought to keep ...nted to just ignore everyone... *She has no right to do ...he doesn't understand what I need.*

...ing, I was sad. And when the tears started, they fell ... lash out at someone, anyone. I was so frustrated and full of emotion that I shook from head to toe.

I wanted to run out the door and never return.

Just run and run and run...

I had never experienced anything like this. All the things I had always done to keep things under control were being stripped away. I felt completely and utterly backed into a corner. Thoughts of death seemed comforting.

> The pain of continuing on my path had become greater than the pain of being willing to change.

Up to now, the only emotion I had let Mary see were my tears. I had always been sweetly compliant to her, even in my stubbornness. I always nodded and agreed with her, even when I had no intention of changing, and shared little emotion. If things got uncomfortable, I would simply not speak, just shrugging my shoulders and clamming up.

And then the tears would come.

Tears have always been a part of me. They have betrayed me ever since I was a little girl. They often seemed rogue and out of my control. Now they once again ran down my cheeks as I refused to speak. Covering my face with my hands, I cried uncontrollably. Mary explained that she would go with me to see the doctor; I wouldn't need to go alone.

She let me cry but kept talking until I finally nodded. She was as determined as I was. She wasn't going to give in. I needed to make a choice.

My face in my hands, I thought rapidly. *What choice do I have?* But then my thoughts went to Mary, and I realized she didn't have much choice either. I began to feel compassion for her. Although I hated the pressure she was putting on me, I understood where she was coming from.

I would go see a doctor.

That doctor's visit was the beginning of a real desire for change. As I sat on the examination table, shivering and shaking and utterly humiliated, I finally saw myself as I really was. I was exactly what the doctor wrote on the paper as his diagnosis—*acute anorexia nervosa.*

Head bowed, I listened as Mary and the doctor discussed my continued treatment. I felt closer than ever to rock bottom. Suddenly the doctor turned to me. "Do you like children?" he asked.

Baffled, I answered from the bottom of my heart, "Yes, I love children. I always have."

"Well, the way you are living now, you will never have any," he said bluntly.

His words hit me hard. As my shell fell away, I once again fought tears. I wanted to be a mother someday. I wanted children of my own. Both my husband and I loved children and had talked many times about having a family. It had never occurred to me that my personal choices could ruin that for me and my husband.

I was finally ready to back away from the cliff and listen. The pain of continuing on my path had become greater than the pain of being willing to change.

I was finally open to receiving God's help.

Mentor's Thoughts

Sometimes it hurts to let Jesus shine His light into our hidden, secret places. Satan lies to us and says God will punish us and reject us if we allow our hidden sins to be known. But God doesn't ask us to confess our weaknesses to shame us or to punish us. Instead, He wants to help us. He knows that unless we ask for help to overcome a sinful habit, we will likely keep falling back into that sin.

Sharing our struggles with a trusted parent, minister, or friend is an important step in breaking Satan's power over us. James 5:16 says, "Confess your faults one to another, and pray one for another, that ye may be healed. The effectual fervent prayer of a righteous man availeth much." Hiding our sins sets us up to fail again and again. On our own, we will almost certainly not be strong enough to resist the pull of what our conscience tells us is wrong. We need the help of others. A burden shared is a burden lightened.

If we lock away our struggles and emotions in secret places, we will also shut out other people, even those closest to us. God's Word tells us to "bear ye one another's burdens" (Galatians 6:2) and to "lift up the hands which hang down" (Hebrews 12:12).

Pray for God to send the right person into your life—someone you can trust. Then open your heart to that person. It may feel painful to expose what is hurting you, but in the end, it is worth all the pain.

As you share your pain, speaking it aloud and allowing someone to help you process it, you bring it from a dark, vague memory to the light of reality. It gives you the chance to hear a different perspective on it, and you will be better able to process what is fact and what may not be as it appears. It will help you understand yourself and your experiences.

Most of all, we must remember to share our hurts with our heavenly Father. He is the One we can depend on most of all. Important as it is to share with other people, they are human. And unless they have walked the same pathway, they may not understand.

Imagine a woman who goes for help after years of struggling with depression. She needs the support and prayers of her friends. Some stand by her, but others tell her to "just get over it." She feels hurt and misunderstood.

Or consider the man who reaches out for accountability to overcome his struggle with alcoholism. A friend commits to walking with him but then fails to do his part. He does not realize how desperately his friend needs him and gets preoccupied with his own things.

But don't give up on people just because someone has failed you. Most likely it was not intentional. Just try again!

> A burden shared is a burden lightened.

And remember that God never fails you. He is always faithful. When we go to God with our struggles, He does not condemn us—He convicts. To condemn is to declare to be wrong or guilty, which can fill us with confusion, self-hatred, and despair. God's conviction, however, shows a way forward and gives us hope. We have the assurance that our loving Father will help us live in freedom.

Author Mark Ballenger describes well the difference between condemning and convicting: "One main difference between condemnation and conviction is where they will lead you. Condemnation leads you further away from God towards death. Conviction leads you closer to God and towards life."[1]

God wants to help us, not just make us feel guilty. The Apostle Paul wrote, "There is therefore now no condemnation to them which are in Christ Jesus, who walk not after the flesh, but after the Spirit" (Romans 8:1).

But when God convicts us, we need to be open to what He tells us. Living in faith and obedience to our Father is the only way to true freedom.

---

[1] From the following article: https://applygodsword.com/what-is-the-difference-between-condemnation-and-conviction/.

Writing Out Your Thoughts...

1. How do you view God the Father? Can you believe that He loves you and is not a harsh master?

2. What things in your life might God be asking you to give to Him? In what ways might these things be hurting you?

3. Have you tried on your own to stop doing things you know are wrong or are hurting you? Have you been successful? What have you tried to give up but keep falling back into?

4. Have you ever shared something privately with someone and later found out the person didn't keep your secret? Did it cause you to lose trust in people? What would help you learn to trust again?

5. With whom would you feel safe in sharing your struggles so that person can help you be accountable?

> *If the Son therefore shall make you free, ye shall be free indeed.* John 8:36

Part Three
Grasping for Control

When in the bondage of an eating disorder, giving up control usually means first being caught between a rock and a hard place. Once there is no other way out, no choice but to give up control to others, only then will we grudgingly make some changes.

In this stage, there is a constant searching for a way around, a way to deal with the problems while still grasping for the reins to maintain control. We do what we absolutely must, but we still believe there are certain things we must do to be okay.

In Part Three, Sarah allows others to help—but only to a certain extent. She does what she has to do to achieve the dream of motherhood, but the root of the eating disorder remains deeply hidden.

chapter 8

A Glimmer of Hope

The next four years of my life were a mixture of some successes and many failures. The biggest difference was that I was now acutely aware that I had a problem and needed help. It was a slow process, but gradually I learned to be more willing to accept help.

My husband was a constant steady in my life, and as I finally allowed him closer to my heart, he became my best friend to the point where I became very possessive of him. An unhealthy mind (lacking proper nutrition) can become extremely paranoid, and unknown to me, this is what I was dealing with. Though I loved my husband more than I had ever loved anyone before, I struggled with unreasonable fears. I was afraid he would leave me, that he wouldn't be faithful to me, that he was somehow betraying me...

He saw my obsession with the scale, and though it upset me, he removed it from our home. As I think back to those days, I see that God carried my husband through a very traumatic time. I owe so much to him for his faithfulness and steady love. Although I know I hurt him through my pain, he was never mean or unkind to me.

Many times my mind was too foggy to process more than what lay right ahead of me. I felt so depressed that I didn't want to get up in the morning. And at night, I couldn't sleep without some kind of sleeping pills. As my health became more precarious, it was harder to hide things.

People began noticing that I was struggling, and that irritated me. Proving that I was okay became an obsession. *No one must know that I am going for help!* I was especially paranoid about the church people. I was terrified that they would gossip.

The few friends I had learned to open up to were the only people I trusted. I wanted them to be there for me, so I did all I could to be a good friend. I didn't want them to desert me; I didn't want to be alone.

Five mornings a week I went to Mary's office for a counseling session. She also kept a close watch on my physical appearance. The doctor had prescribed an antidepressant, and when I finally agreed to take it, the depression and foggy thinking started to improve. I was also being treated for a stomach ulcer.

The sessions in Mary's office wore me out. Sometimes it felt like I was getting worse instead of better. But I was determined to hide the fact that anything was wrong, so I continued my full-time job. Though I liked and appreciated Mary, I hated the way she dug into my thought processing. I rebelled against answering the many probing questions as she peeled back layers and layers of faulty thinking. Sometimes I was so frustrated that I resolved never to come back.

But my job was in the balance, and I had made a promise to my husband to get help. I felt caged in. So I grudgingly kept returning to that little office every weekday morning.

But motivating me more than anything else was a constant thought in my head: *I want to be a mother…*

This was a difficult time for me. I had never, even from a little girl, learned to share what was bothering me. I had stuffed things down for so long that getting it to come out in words seemed impossible. It felt like using a pry bar inside my heart and mind.

To my shame, I had earlier made snide remarks about people needing depression medication or counseling. Now I was the one needing help, and I could only imagine what people were saying. I felt helpless, exposed, ruined. I could do nothing but watch as my critical attitude and lofty opinion of myself came crashing down around me.

Looking back, I can see it more clearly now as a deep-rooted pride and control issue—a result of a heart unwilling to make a complete surrender. I had become so astute at playing the game of "being who I have to be" that I had no idea who I really was.

> God can only work in a fully surrendered heart.

About a year after I made that first visit to see the doctor, I suffered severe cramps. I was having a miscarriage. Though it was extremely difficult for me, it gave me hope. *Maybe I can be a mother after all.* That tiny seed of hope sparked in me an even deeper desire to fight my illness.

It is hard to describe the weeks and months of coming out of the worst of my anorexia and starting to feel better. I look back on it now with a sort of sad fondness, knowing that God took good care of me even when I had no desire to take care of myself. I don't know why He extended so much grace when I played with so much danger. Although I don't understand all the reasons I went so far into the wrong ditch, I see clearly that God was right there with me.

If I could only have grasped how much He loves me. If I could only have learned early in life to trust Him. And not only Him, but the people He sent to help me.

Then I wouldn't have had to walk alone.

A Glimmer of Hope

You would think that after I was so low and started getting better, I would never have wanted to return there again. That I would have reached out openly for help in dealing with my emotions. That instead of hiding my struggles, I would have shared openly and honestly so I could break free from the bondage that came from my secrecy.

But old habits die hard.

And I still had a big lesson to learn: God can only work in a fully surrendered heart.

When we try to hide things, we miss out on many of God's blessings. We remain in the foyer of God's will, so to speak. And unless something changes, my friend, we will remain in the foyer and never get close to the sanctuary of the heart of God.

Only with true surrender—opening wide our hearts, casting aside all our pride, and acknowledging our bondage—can we step into the sanctuary. As we do so, we will find a fulfillment we will never, ever find in the foyer.

Why? Because God's heart is in the sanctuary. That is where we can drink more fully of God's intense love and grace. It is the closest a child of God can get to Him while on this earth. It is a place of beauty, warmth, and compassion. As we learn to know the Father, it brings a settled mind and a sense of peace. It gives us the knowledge that, no matter what, God is our refuge. "Though he slay me, yet will I trust in him" (Job 13:15).

Don't settle for foyer living. Let God look inside the dark corners of your heart. And no matter the cost or the fear, show Him everything you have kept hidden. Hold nothing back. Then step into the sanctuary and be wrapped in the beauty of God's love for you. Allow Him to carry away the shame and the pain.

I lived in the foyer for quite some time. And honestly, God used me there. He gave me many blessings and preserved my soul. I knew Him as God, but not as my Father. I looked on longingly from a distance, but I never quite trusted Him.

It was years before I was willing to surrender everything and learn what life with my Father is like—in the sanctuary.

Mentor's Thoughts

It is possible to ask Jesus into your heart but never let Him in farther than just inside the door. In John 14:6, Jesus says, "I am the way, the truth, and the life: no man cometh unto the Father, but by me." If we never allow access to our inner heart, we can never come close to the sanctuary of the Father's heart.

Why are we afraid to let Jesus have full control of our hearts? What is the root of the fears that keep us from the Father's heart? There are several possibilities:

Immaturity: Young children do not always understand what they hear about God. I remember a story a friend told me. As a little girl, she heard the minister at church talking about not wearing the world's fashions. He specifically mentioned the white shoes that were stylish at the time. But because of his Dutch accent, she understood it as "wide shoes." Imagine her horror when her mom took her shoe shopping and told her they must get wide shoes for her feet. She felt shame and embarrassment to be wearing something so worldly that others at church would see.

This is just an example of how a young mind can skew and misunderstand what it hears. Certain Bible verses can also sound condemning if they are not explained on a child's level.

As we grow and develop, our understanding needs to mature as well. When we ask Jesus into our heart, God's

Spirit helps us understand His Word. But we need to take time to read the Bible, to hear God's Word being preached, and to talk to other Christians. In this way, our understanding will be brought to maturity.

Immunity: Another reason we may not invite Jesus to take full control is that we become calloused to the Word of God. Many of us grew up in Christian homes and heard the Gospel preached for as long as we can remember. This is a great blessing that we should never take for granted, but it can also bring an immunity to God's Word.

Just as our bodies become immune to viruses by being exposed to them, so we can become immune to the powerful Word of God and no longer be affected by it. Constantly hearing Bible stories and being surrounded by the Word should draw us closer to God, but sometimes it can become ordinary and cause a coldness in our heart that can only be broken by fervent prayer.

> If we never allow access to our inner heart, we can never come close to the sanctuary of the Father's heart.

Growing up in Christian homes has the potential to leave us with the false belief that we can "inherit" Christianity. We need to understand that no matter how carefully we have lived, no matter how "good" we have been, we still need to repent of our sinful nature and personally ask Jesus into our heart. We cannot inherit our parents' faith. Each of us must make a personal choice to come to the Father.

Nourishing Our Brain

The foggy thinking Sarah mentioned is a common result of improper food intake. Our brain is an amazing creation that needs to be nourished as the Designer created it to be. Just as a plant needs water and proper nutrients to grow, our brain needs to be nourished properly to function as it should.

Feeding the body junk food will both weaken the immune system and hinder our ability to think clearly. God has designed us so that our physical, mental, and emotional parts are intricately interwoven. If our physical body is worn down by lack of proper nutrition, our brain will not function properly, affecting our ability to deal with our emotions.

Proper nutrition has many parts, including carbohydrates, fat, protein, and fiber. All have their God-given role in keeping a body healthy. Completely cutting out any of them will have a detrimental effect on our health.

Protein, for instance, is an important building block in maintaining emotional stability. The body uses protein to create the amino acids necessary to produce neurotransmitters such as serotonin, which is responsible for many aspects of our emotional and physical health. A lack of it leads to a myriad of emotional issues, including depression, brain fog, obsessive thinking, paranoia, insomnia, and others.

Medication

When a body becomes depleted of necessary nutrients, medication is sometimes required to bring the brain's biological factors back into balance. Symptoms like depression, anxiety, foggy thinking, and low energy will be relieved as the proper medication (under a doctor's care) balances out the brain's neurochemical and hormonal connections.

The physical, mental, and emotional healing necessary for recovery is an exhausting journey, so there is no shame in accepting needed medications to get back on track.

Our body is created in a wonderful way, and God wants to help us care for it. "For ye are bought with a price: therefore glorify God in your body, and in your spirit, which are God's" (1 Corinthians 6:20).

Writing Out Your Thoughts...

1. Sarah's dream of motherhood was being threatened by the choices she was making. What important thing is your eating disorder (or other form of bondage) taking from you?

2. Do you ever feel foggy in your mind? Do you ever feel like you are far away even when in a crowd? What do you think causes that?

3. Do you struggle to fall asleep at night? What happens in your thoughts if you are awake late at night? Does it help to pray? Do you think God hears you?

4. Do you think it is okay to take depression medication if you are struggling to think clearly? Have you or someone you know ever made fun of people who need counseling or medication to help them cope mentally? How can this attitude hurt people who really need help?

5. How do you think pride, fear, or shame can keep people from asking for help when they can't cope on their own? Does pride ever keep you from admitting you aren't strong enough to beat your addiction by yourself? What does it mean to be humble?

> *A man's pride shall bring him low: but honour shall uphold the humble in spirit.* Proverbs 29:23

chapter 9

Hidden Rooms

Slowly but surely my life was changing—in many beautiful ways. Even though I describe it to you as "foyer living," my life was much better than what it had been. I was learning to love and laugh in a new way. And yet I would like to present it with a warning.

I was blessed abundantly. I was so humbled by these blessings that many times I found myself waiting for the other shoe to drop. I lived in gratitude to God because I realized I was so undeserving. Since I still didn't have a very clear view of God and salvation, I continued to hold Him a little at arm's length. But I knew now that self-hatred was sin and not humility, and I was open to advice in gaining freedom from some of my self-destructive behaviors.

As Mary continued to counsel me, she grew discouraged at how difficult it was for me to open up. Our sessions often ended in frustration for both of us. Not ready to give up, she pursued permission from her superiors to come to my house to see if that would relax me enough to share. She went above and beyond to help me be comfortable. It helped so much, but only to a point.

A new world opened when I realized that emotions need to be processed in a healthy way. We can't just stuff our feelings down and self-talk our way out of them. I learned to share with my husband, to be more responsible in the basics of caring for my body, and to talk when I was struggling. I learned to be more open with friends and to be honest if I needed prayer. It was like starting first grade in the emotional side of my life.

Mary often had me look at a chart to help me identity my feelings. I can close my eyes today and see the little yellow faces: sad, happy, concerned, angry, depressed, indifferent, etc. She soon learned that the "indifferent" face was the one I chose when I didn't understand or when I didn't feel like sharing.

But Mary and I always seemed to come to a point where we hit a wall. I had come such a long way that I didn't worry about it a lot, as I had found some healing. I honestly believe now that maybe I wasn't ready yet for the sanctuary—I had more to surrender.

My joy overflowed when God blessed me with my first baby—and then five more over the coming years. I fell in love with each child and thrived in being a mother. I wrapped my heart around these lovely children in a way I didn't know was possible.

Mary continued to counsel me for several more years, and I thank God for using her to help me stop many of my destructive choices. Through her counsel and guidance, I recognized the sin of some of my behaviors and learned how to express happiness, joy, and love. I saw clearly that I cannot walk alone—that I needed other people to help me. I also recognized that medication may be necessary at times for a person to function normally.

Mary tried to find the "real me" as I put on a front to portray who I thought I must be. When she questioned me, my answers were always "correct" but not necessarily honest. She called me her little sister and treated me just like that. She was never threatening but always kind and persistent.

I look back at those years with much fondness, because I was blessed in a way I had never thought I would be—I was a mother! It was a dream I thought had been lost. I loved my children deeply, and through them I found hope and a reason to live. I grieved openly over the three miscarriages I experienced, and each time I had a distinct setback in my emotional and physical health. But I now had friends who had gone through similar experiences, and I bonded with them in a way I had never done before.

Time and again, I balked at my need for medication. I would stop taking the antidepressants and end up struggling. I was determined to do it on my own.

Gradually I found myself stronger, and my times with Mary grew less frequent. We became just friends and then acquaintances as my life moved in a different direction. By the books, I was a success case. I had completed what was required and was marked healed.

But now for the warning. Through those years, there was an important part in which I failed—something I ignored.

As we seek healing, we must keep a close watch on our emotions and belief systems. Are they being molded by God, or are they still stunted and immature? Are they still tangled up, with a focus on ourselves? We must take them to God for evaluation and then pray for discernment to see them through His eyes. Above all, we must be honest and transparent!

> I saw clearly that I cannot walk alone—that I needed other people to help me.

We must follow every rope in our mind to look for these tangles. And when we find one, we must stay with it until we fully understand why it is tangled.

Hidden Rooms

I didn't. And I paid for it.

When I got to the place where I could function, I did what too many people do—I ignored the tangles that I knew were still there and turned my focus elsewhere. Instead of bringing my thoughts and emotions to God to be further transformed, I ignored them. I knew I was still hiding some things, but I was tired of thinking about it. I was fine now.

In my desire to just be normal, I wanted that part of my past to be buried and gone. I never wanted to look at it again.

I knew all about anorexia now and had a healthy fear of it. And I wanted it out of my mind. I wanted to say, "I'm healed; it's all behind me." I wanted to wash my hands, turn tail, and run. Even when I tentatively shared bits and pieces with others to help them through anorexia, I did it with a fear of getting too close.

As a mother now, I was determined to be the very best. Through some distorted thinking, I decided God had me on trial; if I didn't perform correctly, He might take my blessings from me. This immature thought tangle was a carryover from a childhood steeped in trying desperately to be good enough for God.

Instead of evaluating my immature emotions under the light of God's Word, I looked the other way. I didn't want to fight that part of me anymore, so I created a world in which I would be safe. But I wasn't being honest.

I still struggled with depression at times, especially if I was alone or sad, so I gathered friends in droves. I reached out to many, many people, sending cards and making phone calls, trying to fill that place inside me that might take over if I wasn't careful. I was doing the same thing I had done as a teen, but in a little different way. Since I had learned the art of being more open, I really loved these people, and they filled a part of me that needed comfort.

I was fun and friendly—and freely discussed my experiences as a mom. My children were my life, and I loved it. Through my counseling sessions, I had learned how to get others to share with me, and I loved how that affirmed me. I enjoyed having many friends who considered themselves a best friend. I craved their friendship and found that I desperately needed their acceptance and affirmation. Little did I realize I was using these friendships to fill a place in my life that belonged only to God.

But despite my new openness to others, a certain wall was still there. There were eating disorder things I had never completely dropped, things I never openly admitted. Deception was still my default. In times of stress, I still struggled to keep my food and not purge. Because I knew where anorexia had taken me, I didn't want to abstain from eating like before—so I ate when necessary. But instead of learning about health and proper food intake, I simply avoided any focus on food at all.

It didn't work. What had been anorexia just found a new expression.

Because I had not followed the roots of every tangled web in my mind and had ignored my immature emotions, I found myself bulimic—which is a cycle of bingeing and purging. I would go for weeks abstaining from any of these behaviors, then go for weeks wallowing in it. The signs of a raw and bleeding throat would bring me to a halt, trembling in fear and horrified shame, and I would once again make a determined effort to stop. During those times, I felt so much hatred for myself that I questioned my salvation and found myself uncertain about God.

Because of these unhealthy behaviors, I was restless at night and couldn't sleep well. I soon fell into the habit again of taking medication to sleep. Since I portrayed a confident "I'm okay" attitude to others, I had no accountability from them.

I saw these behaviors as wrong, but I felt trapped. After all, I was healed, right? How could I admit that I really wasn't? Occasionally I would be confronted by my husband and had to admit my failures. But slowly, as sin does, I slipped into hiding it from him again. I didn't want to hurt him; I loved him too much. He was so kind and good—and had already been through so much because of me...

I was now on the heavy side physically, weighing more than I had ever imagined I would. I didn't spend much time thinking about it, as it would take me days to recover if I did. But how could I tell people about my new eating disorder? They could easily see that I was no longer anorexic. It was obviously a thing of the past.

But it had only changed faces. I was still operating in an eating-disordered lifestyle. A huge, tangled part of my thinking was still controlling too much of me.

When I looked in the mirror and saw a puffy face and a body too fat, I loathed what I saw. But I quickly put it out of mind. If I ignored it, I could pretend it wasn't there—until I had to make a new dress or get ready to go away. Then I would change from one dress to another... to another. Shame flooded every part of my being as I saw that no matter what I wore, I couldn't look thin. Sometimes by the time I had settled on a dress, I was physically sick and battling a migraine. Deep shame would settle over me, but I did my best to cover it. I was a mother now; I needed to be okay. I didn't want to hurt my children.

> We have to own it—look ourselves full in the face and admit it. No excuses, no crutches.

There were also good things in my life. I loved God and felt a desperate need for Him. I loved my husband and children and threw my heart and soul into mothering. I was also a good friend and listener. These were things I liked about myself, so these were the things I focused on.

But during the quiet times when I was alone, I struggled with serious discouragement. I recognized the effort it took to keep many of my friendships alive, and it made me question if these friends really loved me. I felt overwhelmed by the very friendships I thought I needed for my fulfillment.

Unknowingly, I was doing the same thing as before—making myself who I thought I should be. But I didn't share these struggles with others; I was too afraid of letting people see an area of me that looked broken.

And because of that, I could only enter the foyer of God's will for me.

God wants so much more for us than simple foyer living.

No matter what you are facing or how hard it is, my plea is to follow through to the end—get to the tangled places in your life and your mind and be transparent before the Lord. Recognize each area of weakness and be willing to admit it. This will open the door for the help you need.

We cannot ignore our weaknesses and find freedom. Nor can we blame others. We have to own it—look ourselves full in the face and admit it. No excuses, no crutches. Hiding certain areas of our life just doesn't work. It's like the root of a weed—if there are pieces lingering, it will come back.

The Bible says, "For nothing is secret, that shall not be made manifest; neither anything hid, that shall not be known" (Luke 8:17). These hidden things separate us from God and His plan for us. It doesn't mean He doesn't love us, but He wants all of us, not just some parts.

Ephesians 4: 22-32 covers so much:

> That ye put off concerning the former conversation the old man, which is corrupt according to the deceitful lusts; and be renewed in the spirit of your mind; and that ye put on the new man, which after God is created in righteousness and true holiness.
>
> Wherefore putting away lying, speak every man truth with his neighbour: for we are members one of another. Be ye angry, and sin not: let not the sun go down upon your wrath: neither give place to the devil. Let him that stole steal no more: but rather let him labour, working with his hands the thing which is good, that he may have to give to him that needeth.
>
> Let no corrupt communication proceed out of your mouth, but that which is good to the use of edifying, that it may minister grace unto the hearers. And grieve not the holy Spirit of God, whereby ye are sealed unto the day of redemption. Let all

bitterness, and wrath, and anger, and clamour, and evil speaking, be put away from you, with all malice: and be ye kind one to another, tenderhearted, forgiving one another, even as God for Christ's sake hath forgiven you.

This explains so clearly why we can't allow things to fester in our lives. Paul is telling us not to let lying, anger, thievery, evil communication, sin, bitterness, and such things into our lives because they will separate us from God. This is not because God wants to punish us but because of His love. He knows that when we give place to these things, we will experience foyer living. We will miss out on the beauty of complete openness in Christ and lose out on His peace.

I hadn't yet learned to know the heart of God—that I don't need to make myself into some wonderful person others will like. I hadn't learned that He wants me to be who He made me to be and nothing more.

He wanted me to come just as I am—to step into the sanctuary and let Him have full control.

An open heart with no hidden rooms is the only atmosphere where God can fully heal.

Mentor's Thoughts

In the Bible, God experiences emotion. We read of His love, His anger, His compassion... Since we are created in the image of God,[1] emotions are an important part of our lives. Just as our mind enables us to think and our will enables us to choose, our emotions help us respond. But like our mind and will, our emotions must be brought into subjection to God's control.

The problem is that feelings are fickle, and we cannot base our

---

[1] Genesis 1:27

decisions on how we feel. Feelings must always be examined under the light of truth. Is what we are feeling based on truth? Can we really trust a "gut feeling" about a person or event? Not always. Emotions are a gift from God, but if they are not under His control, they can lead us astray.

What can we do when negative feelings become too heavy to carry, and we don't understand the feelings of sadness, anger, or fear that envelop us? What if our sensitive nature feels these more deeply than others? Too often we choose to stuff these negative feelings down and lock them up. Sadly, this will also lessen our ability to feel positive emotions, and we won't experience joy and love the way God created us to feel them.

When emotions are repressed, they never go away. It is like having a box deep inside with a lock on it. Time after time, the painful emotions are stuffed down, and the lid is slammed shut. The problem is, at some point the box can no longer hold the emotions and they will begin to spill out.

> Emotions are a gift from God, but if they are not under His control, they can lead us astray.

Emotional healing is a difficult and confusing journey, but it is the only way to find peace deep inside your heart and soul.

Three Wrong Choices...

There are many wrong ways to respond to painful emotions. Most of them, however, fit somewhere in the following three categories:

1. Responding with anger, impatience, or another strong emotion. This emotional turmoil is usually flung at the people nearest to us, creating resentment, grudges, and bitterness.

2. Stuffing it down inside and refusing to think about it or talk about it. This causes feelings of guilt, self-loathing, and condemnation. The repressed emotions keep multiplying and festering until they cause physical, emotional, and psychological problems.

3. Wallowing in the hurt and feeling sorry for ourselves. This leads to a "poor me" mentality. Such a person is likely to become bitter, wounded, and overly sensitive.

But it doesn't have to be this way.

The God-Way

God has a much better way for us to respond to unpleasant emotions. He wants us to hold them, allow ourselves to feel them, and then examine them in the light of His Word.

As each painful emotion is run through the filter of God's Word, we are enabled to make deliberate choices—first to give it to our Father, and then to discern what our God-centered response should be. The difficult part of this is learning to "surf the urge."[2]

This means that instead of immediately reacting to a negative emotion, we will ride out the feeling before choosing how to react.

The only way this can work is if we become so familiar with God's Word that it becomes a part of us. Choosing to feel our emotions and then give them to God is not an easy discipline, but with a lot of practice, it becomes easier.

How might this look?

- If you are feeling lonely, you might quote Hebrews 13:5: "For he hath said, I will never leave thee, nor forsake thee."

---

[2] The term "surf the urge" comes from the book *8 Keys to Recovery from an Eating Disorder* by Carolyn Costin and Gwen Schubert Grabb, copyright 2012.

- When you are afraid, you will think of a verse like, "The Lord is my helper, and I will not fear what man shall do unto me" (Hebrews 13:6).
- When you feel heavy burdens, your mind might go to 1 Peter 5:7: "Casting all your care upon him; for he careth for you."

God's Word is full of verses like this—for any kind of emotion we might have. One verse that is a great filter for our thought life is Philippians 4:8: "Finally, brethren, whatsoever things are true, whatsoever things are honest, whatsoever things are just, whatsoever things are pure, whatsoever things are lovely, whatsoever things are of good report; if there be any virtue, and if there be any praise, think on these things."

This verse is so powerful, so complete. As we meditate on its truths, it will change us. It will make real the truth of Psalm 119:11: "Thy Word have I hid in mine heart, that I might not sin against thee."

Being There for Our Children

As parents, we are only human. Sometimes it is our own weak areas that cause damage to our children, but other times it is simply the fallen world in which we live. We cannot keep our children from all pain and difficulty, but there are things we can do to help them.

One way we can give our children the tools to cope with life is to help them understand emotions. They should not only be aware of their own emotions but also those of other people. This will help them realize how other people's emotions often cause them to act as they do.

While they are still young, we can help our children by putting a name to their feelings. Are they *disappointed* because they cannot go to Grandma's house or *sad* because the kitten died? Are they *ashamed* because someone teased them about something or *angry* because someone took their toy? Are they *afraid* of the thunderstorm?

Giving the feelings a name is only the first step. They also need to be taught what to do with the feelings. Sometimes just having a trusted adult show understanding is enough for a child to let go of negative emotions and move on. But sometimes we need to take them step by step through the feelings to understand the proper response. They need to know it is okay to cry tears of sadness and disappointment. It is okay to *feel*. The important thing is what we do with the feelings.

God has called us as parents to guide our children in this way. But first we need to examine our own lives. How do we handle negative feelings? Do we understand what we are feeling—and why? Do we know what to do with it? Are we able to show our grief and tears in a healthy way? Are we humble enough to admit when we react badly to a negative emotion?

If we have never learned to understand and process our own feelings, we can't show our children the healthy way to do it. When we fall for the lie that emotions are bad and must always be repressed, our negative emotions will most likely eventually be manifested as anger. They will cause untold problems to us and to others—physical, mental, emotional, and spiritual.

As conservative Christians, it is part of our teaching to keep our emotions in check. This can be good if it is not taken too far. We are called to a life of moderation and self-discipline. But if we fall off the road into the other ditch of not allowing any emotional expression, we become unbalanced. It is not the way God made us.

God's Word has a wonderful answer when we have burdens: "Come unto me, all ye that labour and are heavy laden, and I will give you rest" (Matthew 11:28).

Writing Out Your Thoughts...

1. When you feel emotions that are intense or confusing, what do you do? With which of the three wrong ways are you most likely to respond?

2. What keeps you from getting closer to God? What scares you about Him?

3. In what ways do you try to create a "safe" world where you do not need to deal with sadness, fear, or anger? How has that worked for you?

4. What are things you have learned to focus your energy on so you do not have to feel the pain inside or think about things that bring negative feelings?

5. What dreams do you have that you are afraid to hope for?

> *Be careful for nothing; but in every thing by prayer and supplication with thanksgiving let your requests be made known unto God. Philippians 4:6*

To Ponder

Do you ever feel like God has you on trial? That all the blessings He wants to give you are dependent on your performance? That if you don't "measure up," God will somehow punish you?

When bad things happen, do you believe it is because you failed in some way or displeased God?

chapter 10

You Cannot Get Around It

In the busyness of motherhood, I had little time for self-focus. In some ways, this was a good thing, but it also prolonged any chance of complete healing. As the years rolled by and we faced many new things as a family, I grew in a number of areas. God worked quietly in my life to bring about spiritual maturity, and I learned many things about Him through my children.

But many of my struggles with food remained unresolved. I placed the whole struggle into a box in my mind and tried to lock the lid tightly. I realized it wasn't taken care of, because sometimes the lid burst open and caused trouble. But most of the time I could ignore it. A time or two I tried dieting but with no success. It always triggered the explosion of that box, and I could see it would

> You cannot ignore a box like this and live in freedom. You simply cannot.

not work. So I would back away and refuse to face it. Over and over, in times of stress, I found myself falling back into old habits.

During those years, I was brought face to face with my issue of pride, and I recognized the damage I did when I refused to ask for help or advice. In addition to learning from my children, watching my husband be a good father also worked wonders in my heart.

When my youngest was a year old, I again fought my need for medication. I thought maybe the time was right to end it. But instead of my usual "I just won't take it" attitude, I prayed and talked to my husband, seeking his permission. He wanted me to do it with a doctor's advice, so I made an appointment.

Ever since I had been diagnosed as anorexic, the doctors had always weighed me backwards on the scale. I had grown to like this, and all through my child-bearing years I had chosen not to see the number. It just worked better that way.

At this doctor's appointment, I didn't request that—and I was in for a shock. The number that popped up on the scale appalled me, filling me with such revulsion that I felt sick. I hid my reaction as I listened carefully to his instructions on how to wean myself off the medication. I even braved a few questions about losing weight, which he really encouraged.

I left the appointment with a steely determination—I had reached my limit. I would not gain one more pound. Something was going to change. By the time I got home from that appointment, there was no turning back. I had no deliberate plan, but I knew in my heart that I would one day be thin again.

But I knew I had to be careful. I loved my husband and my six children, and I didn't want to do the things I had done before. I wanted to be a good example and do things in a healthy way. I started with the medication. Slowly, per the doctor's orders, I backed off the pills until I was free. I was very hesitant. One month...two...three...It was working! I noticed very little shift in my mental state, which delighted me in a way I cannot describe. I felt more energetic and noticed things changing a little in my emotions. I felt stronger feelings—deeper love but also deeper pain.

I knew I had to tread carefully, as a wide swing of highs and lows in emotions had started my earlier downward spiral. After taking some natural products for about six months, I felt things leveling out more. Along with the ability to feel greater joy came the ever-present tears when my heart was touched. It felt a little like walking a tightrope—I had agreed to go back on medication if it didn't work, but I was so determined to make it work that I willingly faced my emotions in a way I hadn't for years.

I heard about a group of ladies from church that met every so often for accountability to lose weight and be healthy. With trepidation, I joined them.

As I allowed myself to look at food realistically after all these years of avoidance and distorted views, I could scarcely believe how off track I had been. This area of thinking was so tangled I could hardly see through it. Learning both the positives and negatives of food really overwhelmed me, and I came home from those first meetings with a headache and many doubts about my ability to comprehend it. I felt so ignorant. It was like my mind was stuck at a second-grade level.

But as I stayed with it, I started to see some success. Although I refused to weigh myself, I followed the suggestions of my accountability group and soon began to notice positive things. My dresses were looser and fit nicer, and I felt better. I grew excited about the possibilities and became very determined. I went above and beyond what was required each week.

Although I tried desperately to stay away from all eating disorder habits, slowly but surely I found myself battling them again. Fearing another crash, I took an honest look into the future for the first time. *What will happen if I don't share my struggle? Where will this pathway lead?*

I believe God allows us windows into the future at times, and He did this for me. As I saw my downward spiral, I knew I needed to change. I realized where I was and where I was headed—and that I could not do it alone. I felt a clear nudge from God, as if He were telling me, "Do whatever it takes to be safe. Don't give in. Do not hide this."

I had no other choice—I had to open that yucky box I had hidden in my life and allow others to help me sort through it. I knew that unless I was willing to be honest, I would end up right back where I had started. With my responsibilities as a wife and mother, I certainly had no desire to go there again! My husband was well acquainted with my struggle, but I wanted to spare him the responsibility of monitoring my food intake. Doing that seemed to pull both of us down.

At the next two health meetings, I was determined to share my struggle but left without opening up. I was too ashamed. I was afraid of how they would respond and that they might think me weird or something. Rolling through my head were all the reasons I dared not be honest.

But by the next meeting, I was ready. The past two weeks had been a disaster. I had faced the worst struggles since I had stopped seeing Mary. I had battled with every eating disorder tendency I had ever faced and had failed miserably. I had done everything I thought I would never do again.

With much shame and humility, I finally shared parts of the truth. I watered it down some because I didn't know what they would say. I trembled in fear of being rejected, but in a beauty seen only in God's true followers, these ladies offered me a ray of hope. There was no condemnation, no shame. They shared my tears, and I sensed a deep love from all of them that was beyond what I had expected.

But the more I had to share my failures, the more I sensed their growing concern. I didn't blame them as they really didn't understand, but I felt myself floundering and became less and less honest. By giving in to my fears, I was again ignoring the box I had so purposefully hammered shut in the recesses of my mind.

But you cannot ignore a box like this and live in freedom. You simply cannot.

I cannot overstate the importance of walking the entire way through healing until you understand what went wrong and what you need to do to be free. Otherwise you will end up fighting the same battles repeatedly. Follow through and be purposeful in whatever it takes. Go to God in prayer and trust that He can help you walk in total freedom.

Believe in God's power and healing. He can heal any wounded places you have inside.

"But Sarah, you have no idea what I have been through," you might say. And you are right. I don't know your story—your pain. I don't know the evil that wounded you or the trauma that broke your heart and causes your mind to struggle. I don't know your fears or your past.

But I know my Father. And He is able to do "exceeding abundantly above all that we ask or think."[1]

That mountain ahead of you? If you push through until you get to it, you may find it is only an anthill. Whatever it is, God can make a way through. He is able.

My friend, grab hold of His outstretched hand and believe this truth: He. Is. Able.

Mentor's Thoughts

Sarah shares how her understanding of health and nutrition was stuck at about a second-grade level. This can happen in different areas of our life when we shut down or fail to think logically. For someone with an eating disorder, the fear of food becomes an obsession until even basic nutrition is not understood. When an area like this becomes stunted, we must be willing to "go back to school" and start where our learning stopped.

---

[1] Ephesians 3:20

Maybe it's a bit like my friend's son. She was homeschooling him and by sixth grade it became obvious that he could no longer just be pushed through math. Testing showed that his math skills were at a first-grade level. They needed to go back to first-grade math, even though he was twelve years old. Going back to the basics helped him learn it correctly, and before long he was back to his grade level and doing well.

When our comprehension becomes stuck at a foundational level, we need to go back to where our thinking got stuck and twisted. This may be fears and trauma, or it may be our understanding of God. Just as my friend's son needed a teacher/mother to guide him, we may need a friend/mentor to guide us through our emotional learning process. An important element in this is seeking accountability from a trusted source—someone who can help us sort through our wrong thinking and point us to the truth.

> If we truly want to walk in freedom, we must choose the pathway God shows is necessary.

What Is Accountability?

Accountability implies a willingness to accept responsibility for one's actions. But it only works if we are willing to accept it. Why does the thought of being accountable to another often cause us so much anxiety? Could it be that our attitude about being accountable is wrong? What if we would choose to be accountable without being forced to do it?

It can be difficult to choose to be accountable to another. We often look at it as something we take from someone else, or they take from us. If we are accountable to someone, do we wait to comply until they "check up on us"? If that's the case, we are likely to hope they won't ask—and we view them as policemen out to catch us.

But what if we would change the way we look at this? What if we realized that holding our life as an open book will help us gain victory over temptation? What if we put our areas of struggle out into the open without any coercion? We do it because we want to.

Doing this takes a deep desire to live in freedom. We are no longer trying to see what we can get away with but are willingly placing ourselves in front of another's inspection to keep us from falling.

Many of life's choices come down to a simple question: What do I really want?

We have two choices. We can either choose our own pathway and accept where it takes us, or we can choose our destination and accept the pathway we must take to get there.

If we truly want to walk in freedom, we must choose the pathway God shows is necessary. With an eating disorder—and other forms of bondage—the most direct pathway to freedom is the path of choosing accountability.

Writing Out Your Thoughts...

1. Do you see the same steely determination in yourself that Sarah described? In what ways are you different?

2. What are your greatest fears in sharing your inner struggles and shame? What things are you blocking out?

3. What is keeping you from complete healing? Do you believe it is possible to be free? What do you think freedom might look like?

4. When you fail, do you share honestly? How do you feel when you keep it hidden?

5. How could sharing help you have victory?

> *Confess your faults one to another, and pray one for another, that ye may be healed. The effectual fervent prayer of a righteous man availeth much. James 5:16*

chapter 11

Who Am I?

Who am I?

It may seem like a simple question, and I might answer flippantly with my name, my parents' names, or even my grandparents' names. I might give my skin color, my age, my nationality, or what church I go to.

But who am I? Really?

I had to face this question, and you will too.

As I floundered to stay the course of losing weight, flipping back and forth between my eating disorder and a determination to not spiral out of control, I felt myself coming to a crossroads. But as I looked this way and that, I couldn't see through the haze of my own world.

Unless you have been there, you may not know what I mean when I say "haze," but that is the best word I can think of to describe it.

On one hand, I was a competent adult. I was a mother and a wife, doing all the things other godly women were doing. I was a laundry woman, a school mom, a gardener, a cook, and a cleaning lady, to name only a few. These were things I loved, and I loved my God and my church. I loved supporting my husband and standing with him. I knew I was blessed, and I was so grateful.

But on the other hand, I was still so confused in certain parts of my mind. These undealt-with areas kept cropping up and frustrating me. I felt guilty and ashamed. I didn't understand how other women could do it. How could they be healthy in body and mind without doing the things I did? *Why do I keep being tempted in areas that frustrate me? Why can't I have victory?* I grappled with discouraging thoughts and didn't know what to do about it... *If only I'd be normal.*

Why can't I figure out how to overcome these things? Why am I this way?

I shared many long talks with a friend, and she encouraged me to go for help or counseling again. I wanted to, but I was afraid people would find out. They might talk, and my husband and children would be hurt because of my struggle.

There was also a fear that I would be pressured to take medication again, and I didn't want that. I thought I could feel God prodding me not to, but how could I be sure?

I prayed for a pure heart. "Search me, O God, and know my heart: try me, and know my thoughts: and see if there be any wicked way in me, and lead me in the way everlasting."[1] It was one of the sincerest prayers I have ever prayed.

One day, in a way I never imagined, I met an older woman who became an important part of God's plan for my life.

Hannah was like me in many ways—sociable and outgoing. As I learned to know her, I found a thoughtful, caring soul under her carefree personality. I'm still not sure why, except that God prompted me, but I started sharing my eating struggles with her. It was always very near the surface

---

[1] Psalm 139:23–24

because I was still on my weight-loss journey.

As Hannah and I started email communication, I found it easier to share my struggles through writing. I wrote and wrote and wrote. Through my fingers poured the years of frustration and humiliation. Hannah always responded positively, never making me feel like a failure. Instead, she offered to hold me accountable in areas I was struggling. She allowed me to be accountable to her in food, exercise, and other things. She read books and learned so many things that she shared with me—things I had refused to look at. Many were simple things: What is protein? Why shouldn't we skip meals? What are empty calories? Why is water so important? What do purging and pills do to your body long-term?

Because of the "haze" I had fought for so long, these things had never even entered my mind. But now the time was right. I was ready to learn—ready to deal with the tangled mess I had hidden for so long. Slowly we came to knot after knot of tangled thinking, and little by little, with much prayer and kindness, Hannah helped me untangle each one until I began to comprehend the truth. Some things seemed so basic, but I needed to start at the beginning.

We started going through several books together, and that's when I came face to face with the question: *Who am I?*

> No matter what label you have been given—anorexic, dyslexic, bossy, slow...God has no limits like this.

What if I no longer had an eating disorder? What if I was completely healed? Did I actually want to be free if I could no longer do the things I was used to? What if I had to let God show me who He made me to be? What if I had to start each day with an open-handed, "Please tell me what I may or may not do today, Lord..."?

That's when I realized that by labeling myself for so many years, I didn't know who I really was. Me—without an eating disorder? What did that even look like? Me—not able to do the things I thought made me lovable and worthy?

I honestly didn't think it was possible to be me apart from these things.

But how often do we limit God by standing in His way? What I share now is with absolute adoration for the One who made me exactly who I am. Although anorexia, bulimia, pride, and a controlling spirit tried to define me—God has redeemed me! I am not those things.

No matter what label you have been given—anorexic, dyslexic, bossy, slow, bipolar, ADHD, sloppy, adopted, orphaned, disorganized, abused... (add your own label to this list), God has no limits like this.

You are not those things. I repeat, "You. Are. Not. Those. Things." God has no labels for you except one.

His child.

You are a beautiful creation. Never let anyone make you feel you are worthless or less meaningful than anyone else. God has made you and you are perfect in His sight.

You are a beautiful, priceless treasure, created to be His child.

Yes, you have faults and failures, but God loves you with an everlasting love. No matter what you are facing—no matter what battle you are in or how hard life is—God is able to bring you freedom. He wants you right next to His heart.

He would have died, my friend, had you been the only one. He loves you. He has a label for you that fits you much better than anything this world can slap on you.

Who am I in Christ? I have finally learned the answer: *I am redeemed, set free, and forgiven. He loves me. I am His.*

And so are you.

Mentor's Thoughts

Who am I?

This is a question most of us will grapple with sooner or later. As we look at the world around us—fashion, sports, music—there are so many interests that clamor for our identity. Many times people choose how to present themselves to the world, but inside they really don't know who they are.

When the appearance of our body, a striving for perfection, or a need for approval becomes an obsession in life, this is the idolatry of self. It is not who God created us to be. We must ask ourselves who we would be if all these "identities" were taken from us. Then we must ask God to show us who He created us to be and who we are in Him.

Put simply, our lives are made up of three main areas of influence: our thoughts and emotions, our relationships with family and friends, and the influence of society around us. Think of it as three circles.

Thoughts, emotions, sensations	Relationships with family and friends	Society and culture, church, work, media

Without a solid foundation of knowing who we are in God's plan, we will try to find our identity within these circles. How we feel will control our choices and decisions. The way family and friends respond to us matters so much that pleasing them and keeping everyone happy is more important than standing for truth.

Rules of Christian living will become a dictator instead of a way to live a simple, godly life. Images seen in the media (magazines, etc.) will become the standard we must achieve to be accepted. The overriding feeling is one of being lost and alone.

Learning to know who God says we are changes the whole picture. These circles will then intertwine, with God as the center anchor.

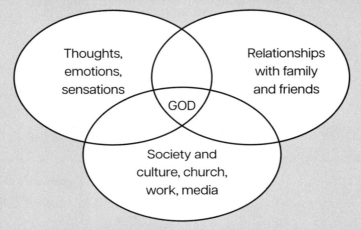

Knowing that God created us and loves us just as we are brings freedom from the need to please and perform for others. One of the hardest steps is learning to accept and love who God made us to be—historically, biologically, genetically, and emotionally. So often we compare ourselves with others and focus on the things we seem to lack. When we do this, we start to hate who we are—our body, our looks, our habits, everything about us. But this is not God's will. After all, he is the One who designed us! Once we learn to love and accept the way God made us, we can allow Him to shape our lives and change our weak spots to look more like Him.

Having a life centered on God will bring inner strength that is no longer swayed by feelings. Even though we will be kind to others, our life is not dictated by whether others are happy with us. We no longer look for acceptance by conforming to the whims or standards of society—or to any other standard than the one set by God's Word. We can experience peace, joy, and security as we rest in knowing we are accepted in Him.

The world says we need to be strong with an inner strength. The problem is, they leave out the Father who created us and loves us. Without God as our center, we are likely to place our identity in self. The three areas of influence become areas to be manipulated to suit our own purposes. We become controlling in our relationships, making sure everyone performs to fit our needs. Church and work become places of power-seeking as we try to control decisions and make sure everything fits into our own mold. We have a feeling of restless discontent unless we are in control.

God is calling us to place our all on His altar of sacrifice and to seek our fulfillment in Him.

You may find, as I did, that God may strip you down to where you feel He is taking away everything that matters. But He wants you to seek fulfillment and identity in Him alone. When we learn this lesson, God will return what we thought had been lost. When He does, we will find that He has given us gold for the worthless plastic toys we gave up.

If we surrender to the Father, He will ever so gently shape us to look like He does. He will make us a new creation in Christ.

> Once we learn to love and accept the way God made us, we can allow Him to shape our lives and change our weak spots to look more like Him.

Writing Out Your Thoughts...

1. List some of your "identities."

2. What are things you have looked to for your identity that may have become a sort of god to you?

3. What do you fear about losing certain parts of these identities?

4. What do you hope to discover about yourself and your personality as you begin the process of letting go? Do you believe it is safe and okay to just be "you"? Why or why not?

5. What are some attributes of God the Father that you want to grow in? Do you really believe He can change you into His image?

> But ye are a chosen generation, a royal priesthood, an holy nation, a peculiar people; that ye should shew forth the praises of him who hath called you out of darkness into his marvellous light: which in time past were not a people, but are now the people of God. 1 Peter 2:9-10

Part Four
Surrendering Control

The most important step in surrendering control is to learn who God really is and to understand His deep love. Only then will it feel safe to trust Him.

The process of understanding what caused an eating disorder requires finding and exposing the roots of the lies that formed it. Going back through this tangled thinking is a painful process and takes much time and compassion.

In Part Four, Sarah starts experiencing the truth that our heavenly Father is love and that He can be trusted. Slowly the lies that bound her are being exposed to the light of God's Word.

Chapter 12

Waiting on the Lord

Healing is never an easy road.

If we break a bone, it takes time, patience, and rest. Healing our mind and emotions is the same. It takes much time and patience.

I heard of a man who suffered from a boil. When he finally went to the doctor, it was so painful and irritated he could hardly walk. The doctor told him they would need to lance the boil and get out the infection before healing could take place. "I'm sorry, sir," the doctor told him. "But I have to hurt you more before you can get better."

That didn't sound very pleasant. More pain? Why not just put on some salve? But that wouldn't work. Unless the festering infection is removed, the boil will only flare up again.

It would need to get worse before it could get better.

That was the place I found myself. Stripped of everything I knew as me, I found myself facing each day with a heavy heart, unsure of anything. The process of removing the damaged thinking and changing it to truth was wearing me down, not only physically but also mentally and emotionally.

Although I had earlier walked the pathway of healing from anorexia, I now realized my healing was far from complete. Like the man's boil, it would have to be lanced. I knew emotional healing was painful and messy, and the thought of walking through that pathway again was overwhelming.

And this time, it was not only anorexia but also bulimia. It brought a lot of shame because I was older now and felt a sense of responsibility to my family. I found it hard to accept. *Why do I still need help like this? Why can't I overcome my problems?*

Thankfully, much of my healing took place in my own home. My email correspondence with Hannah filled many pages. Some days I plowed through with determination, wanting to get through this. Other times I felt discouraged and didn't want to face it.

Through phone calls and emails, I walked back through my tangled thinking. First through the anorexia, then to the bulimia, which was far more shameful to me. With each base we covered, Hannah encouraged me to share with my husband. Although I loved my husband, sharing some of these things with him was really hard. When something was hurting, my nature was to push it down inside. But that was no longer an option.

By now I saw clearly that my eating disorder was a surface manifestation of a deeper heart issue. And I knew I needed to face it.

All of it. Completely.

To do that, I needed to wholly surrender who I wanted to be. I had to say, "Okay, God, help me to be who you made me to be."

It was one of the loneliest times of my life. But it was so important!

God didn't just want my eating disorder handed to Him—He wanted everything. He wanted my need for love and acceptance, my striving for control and reputation…He wanted it all.

I held tightly to verses He gave me in a clear, almost audible way. I found Revelation 3:20-21 a wonderful promise: "Behold, I stand at the door, and knock: if any man hear my voice, and open the door, I will come in to him, and will sup with him, and he with me. To him that overcometh will I grant to sit with me in my throne, even as I also overcame, and am set down with my Father in his throne."

I went from being an outgoing, "make-things-happen" person to simply focusing on caring for my family and myself. It felt like I was slowly being stripped down to nothing. I had nothing to offer or give. I was just doing the bare necessities and sometimes barely that. The work of learning to think in a new way took all my energy.

It took a lot of my focus to eat in a healthy way, with no bingeing or purging, and to exercise safely and sanely. I wanted to be okay for my husband and children, so I tried with all my heart to learn the right way to do these things.

I often had to question my motives. *Why am I doing this? Is it for acceptance from others—or is God asking me to do it? Am I people-pleasing, or am I pleasing God?*

I also had to analyze my emotions. *Why am I feeling angry? Sad? Discouraged? Frustrated? Why am I making a phone call to my friend? Is it for comfort or affirmation? Am I going to her instead of to God?*

When I finally surrendered everything to God, I felt completely barren. I don't say that to discourage anyone but to acknowledge what may happen as you walk through healing. Going back to the tangles took me there in every way, so I actually felt those feelings again. But something was different. Although it felt like a barren valley, I had a sense of hope for the future. I felt the presence of God, and it kept me pressing on.

Some of my friends chose not to stick with me, as I no longer did the right things to please them. When they questioned my motives, certain I was off track, I felt rejected and misunderstood. Always before, I would have bent over backwards to do whatever it took to make sure everyone was happy, but I could no longer do that. For the sake of my husband and family, and to honor God, I simply could not make myself that person anymore.

It felt like God took away my ability to reach out to others. The things I thought I had to do to be loved, I simply couldn't do anymore. Even if I tried, it didn't work out. I discovered I wasn't as quick-witted as I had been; it just wasn't there anymore. Uncertain of anything, I had to rely completely on Him.

I felt Him continually jerking me back. His constant reminders brought me to a stop many times.

I have always been strong-willed, and during this time of darkness I cried out to God in misery. "I came to you for healing, Lord, but here I am—confused, lonely, sad, and misunderstood. Where are you? What do you want from me? Help me see the way... Please, Father."

His answer was always the same. "Keep walking... Wait on me. Be patient. I will be with you."

As I struggled to learn new habits of being healthy, I kept tripping on my stubbornness. Every time I chose not to do what I usually did in stressful times, I had to deal with my emotions. They hit me one after another in waves, like a hurricane. The range of emotions went from one extreme to the next, and it was all I could do to stay on top of them.

God was merciful to me in so many ways through this. Even when my emotions hit me hard, I believe God paced them so I would be okay. Deep down I felt an assurance I had never experienced before—an assurance of His presence. I also had the support of people in my life.

My husband trusted me and tried to understand my struggles. Always kind, he stood up for me when I was misunderstood, taking time to listen to my tears.

My group of ladies from church still supported me in my battles with food, giving me ideas and explaining even the simplest things to me.

They didn't seem to mind that I wasn't perfect, and they often shared their own struggles.

Then there was Hannah, whom God had seemingly given nerves of steel. She remained faithful even when I challenged her or refused to talk. Sometimes I accepted her advice, but other times I tried hard to get around it. She constantly turned me back to God and the Bible. Many an emotional storm was fought with her, and I harbored the fear that she would give up on me—that she would tell me I needed to get help elsewhere. Her answer to that was, "As long as you are making progress and trust me, I will try to help you."

> True friendship isn't about what we do for each other, but about loving each other no matter what.

I also had other friends and family who stuck with me, although I'm sure they didn't always understand. They showed me that true friendship isn't about what we do for each other, but about loving each other no matter what.

For the first time in my life, I surrounded myself with God's Word. To be a fully healthy person, we need God's Word—lots of it. We need it every day, whether or not we feel God's presence.

I set a strict, set-in-stone time for myself to spend with God daily. To this day, I seldom miss it. I can't. I need Him too much.

We all need Him. No matter where we are in our journey, we need Him. We need to set our faces like flint and keep His Word by our side and in our hearts every day.

As I surrounded myself with the Word of God, it became more alive to me. So often when I had read the Bible in the past, I had felt condemned and ashamed. The tangled threads in my mind had warped my ability to comprehend the full scope of who God is. Instead of seeing the hope of the Scriptures, I felt only condemnation.

Waiting on the Lord

Slowly He chiseled away the feelings of unworthiness and replaced them with words of truth. He showed me verses about caring for my body, about hypocrisy, about liars—and He made them real to me. For the first time I saw His love, and this gave me so much hope.

Through His Word, I fell in love with a Father who is more than I ever imagined. He has more than enough power to give us victory. He is more than the approval of man. He is more than any desire of our hearts.

He is everything.

As I wrestled through verse after verse, feeling conviction and applying it to my life, many areas were exposed that needed His touch. As Hebrews 4:12 says, I found God's Word living and sharp, "a discerner of the thoughts and intents of the heart." Changing my way of thinking was hard—and it hurt. But I learned to know God in a new way.

Whenever I would confidently step out in an effort to please people or put on a good front, I felt a prick in my spirit…I couldn't do it. This was hard on me, because as I waited on Him, I realized I might not be as close to these people anymore. God was reshaping me, and I had to allow myself to be molded by Him. To do that, there were things I needed to let go.

My view was still limited at this time—a simple day to day, sometimes hour to hour, walk. I couldn't see more than a step ahead, but God's Word was the Lamp I needed to light my pathway. I questioned and re-questioned my walk, and always God's answer was the same. "Keep walking, and wait on me."

All I could do was fall at His feet in brokenness and pray, "O God, be merciful to me. Make me pure in heart."

And again and again, He opened His arms and showed me His scars. His beautiful scars.

For me.

Mentor's Thoughts

Unless we have some rare genetic abnormality, everyone's brain is structured in a similar way at birth. Our brain is then shaped and developed by the environment we grow up in and the choices we make. A baby cannot choose how she is raised or whether peace or chaos surrounds her. She does not choose whether her parents are loving, gentle, and kind—or harsh, abusive, and negligent. But each of these environments will have an impact on brain development and will shape the way the child learns to think and respond.

But that does not mean we cannot help the way we are. Some people will have more difficulties to overcome, but we all have to choose how we will respond to life. Jesus' words in John 16:33 apply to everyone: "These things have I spoken unto you, that in me ye might have peace. In the world ye shall have tribulation: but be of good cheer; I have overcome the world."

In this verse, Jesus shows us, with two simple words, the only way to overcome—"in me." In Jesus we find the way to health, freedom, and hope. The Apostle Paul tells us in 1 Corinthians 2:16 that if we are filled with the Holy Spirit, we have "the mind of Christ."

Following are some verses in which Paul points out our need for this renewed mind and shows us how to get it:

- "And be renewed in the spirit of your mind" (Ephesians 4:23).

- "And have put on the new man, which is renewed in knowledge after the image of him that created him" (Colossians 3:10).

- "And be not conformed to this world: but be ye transformed by the renewing of your mind, that ye may prove what is that good, and acceptable, and perfect, will of God" (Romans 12:2).

- "Wherefore gird up the loins of your mind, be sober, and hope to the end for the grace that is to be brought unto you…" (1 Peter 1:13).

What exactly does it mean to "gird up the loins of your mind"? In Bible times, men wore long, flowing robes that made it hard to move quickly. If a man needed to run, he would gather up the front of his robe and tie it so it was more like a short pair of pants. This made it easier to move without getting tangled up in the skirt.

Today the phrase means to prepare oneself to deal with a difficult situation, and that is exactly what Paul meant—preparing your mind to respond in the right way to life's circumstances.

Psychology today uses a treatment method called cognitive behavioral therapy (CBT) to identify wrong thinking, immature emotional responses, and destructive behaviors. The patient is then taught to replace these faulty habits with more desirable patterns of thinking and responding. In many ways, this is similar to the "renewing of your mind" spoken of in Romans 12:2.

God calls us to focus on His Word to identify wrong thinking patterns. Where do we start? Ephesians 5:18 gives us an all-important key: "And…be filled with the Spirit." The way to be filled with the Holy Spirit is to ask God to fill us. Luke 11:13 tells us, "If ye then, being evil, know how to give good gifts unto your children: how much more shall your heavenly Father give the Holy Spirit to them that ask him?"

An empty bucket is just a bucket until it is filled with something, then it becomes a carrier of whatever we put in it. Without God, my soul is also an empty shell. But if it is filled with His Spirit, it becomes a carrier of the fruits of the Spirit. Just as water splashes out of a bucket filled with water, so our emotions will splash out of us. If I am filled with negativity, that is what will spill out on others around me. But if I am filled with God's Spirit, good things will spill out.

Renewing the mind is a difficult journey. Our human tendency is to follow our thinking wherever it goes and then deal with the consequences. That is like floating with the current in a swift river, watching for rocks and snags while being swept along. Renewing our mind requires turning around and fighting the current as we head upstream. This takes constant focus and an awareness of the thoughts on which I allow my mind to dwell.

In 2 Corinthians 10:3-5 Paul tells us so clearly, "For though we walk in the flesh, we do not war after the flesh: (for the weapons of our warfare are not carnal, but mighty through God to the pulling down of strong holds;) casting down imaginations, and every high thing that exalteth itself against the knowledge of God, and bringing into captivity every thought to the obedience of Christ."

We see several points here. First, it is a spiritual warfare. Satan knows if he can control our mind, he owns us. But we also see that God is stronger than Satan. We are "more than conquerors through him that loved us" (Romans 8:37).

God has given us power, through His Spirit, to control what we allow our minds to think. We are to make every thought captive to Him. When His Word points out wrong thinking and beliefs, we are called to be obedient in changing the way we think. We can replace faulty thinking with God's way of thinking!

As in any kind of bondage, eating-disordered thinking needs to be changed. This is not easy, but it can be done. Much of this journey requires letting go of control and giving it over to God. It means letting go of the need for perfection and accepting our limitations without feeling shame.

Always remember—how we think is our choice, and how we choose to respond is under our control.

With God's help, we can be "renewed in the spirit of your mind." We can change the way we think.

Checking Our Filters

Whether we realize it or not, we all have a filter of sorts in our mind that determines how we view every thought, word, and image coming through our senses. The question to ask is whether this filter, or worldview, is negative or positive. Is it based on the Word of God or on my own nature and experiences?

Most importantly, is my understanding of God based on a filter of truth? Do I understand Him according to the Word—or is it based on circumstances I have faced?

When childish thinking gets us off track, many times the understanding of God's character becomes skewed. This faulty filter will follow us into adulthood unless it is replaced by the truth of what the Bible says. This may require someone to guide us.

If God is seen as a stern judge who is impossible to please and who rejects us for even the slightest infraction, then Romans 8:1 becomes a verse to fear: "There is therefore now no condemnation to them which are in Christ Jesus, who walk not after the flesh, but after the Spirit." A negatively filtered mind may shrink from this because we start thinking, *But what if I am after the flesh and not after the Spirit? I sometimes do things I shouldn't, so I must be condemned.*

Ephesians 4:30 is another verse that may bring uncertainty and fear to a heart that sees God as stern and judgmental: "And grieve not the holy Spirit of God, whereby ye are sealed unto the day of redemption." Instead of a loving plea from a gentle Father, it becomes a verse that condemns us.

The only way to replace a faulty filter with a clear filter of truth is to immerse ourselves in God's Word every day. The Bible has many verses and passages that can help us learn who God is so we can trust Him.

> How we think is our choice, and how we choose to respond is under our control.

If we feel a fear of God's Word or cringe at the thought of letting Him see into our heart, it is an indication that our filter is faulty. John tells us in 1 John 4:16-19, "God is love; and he that dwelleth in love dwelleth in God...There is no fear in love; but perfect love casteth out fear: because fear has torment...We love him, because he first loved us."

In 2 Timothy 1:7 we read much the same: "For God hath not given us the spirit of fear; but of power, and of love, and of a sound mind."

The fear mentioned in these verses is the strong emotion of being afraid of something. This is the fear that Jesus says He will carry for us.

Another meaning of fear in the Bible is a reverent awe toward a holy God, which we do need. This is not a negative, scary feeling, but one of humble reverence to our Creator—the One who sacrificed His only begotten Son to draw us to Him. He loves us that much.

Writing Out Your Thoughts...

1. Do you see things first as positive or negative? What is your first reaction to someone's words? Do you assume they are for you or against you?

2. Do you normally assume people like you?

3. What or who has influenced your view of God? Do you think your view lines up with the God revealed in Jesus?

4. What do Romans 8:1 and Ephesians 4:30, mentioned above, mean to you? How do they make you feel?

5. If you think of God on His throne and you standing before Him, how does that make you feel?

6. What are you afraid of letting God see in your life? What do you fear Him taking from you if you offer it to Him?

7. How do verses like 1 John 4:16–19 and 2 Timothy 1:7 make you feel? Can you believe or imagine not feeling any fear, but trusting everything to God? What keeps you from this?

> *Peace I leave with you, my peace I give unto you: not as the world giveth, give I unto you. Let not your heart be troubled, neither let it be afraid.* John 14:27

Doors in My Heart

"No…Stop…Lord, don't take me there…
That aching darkness filled with despair…
Alone—unloved…so little, afraid…
No way to express it—no one to give aid…

"Please, Lord, no…It's been too many years.
So many times of blocking these tears…
Distorted views, shame-filled anguish…
Surely we don't need to look at this…

"That part seems better left alone,
Stuffed and forgotten until it is gone."
Shaking, quaking…No thought but to hide…
No one…No one dare come inside…

No one ever did…No one ever cared…
And even if they tried, they soon didn't dare…
But now things have changed…hope shines through…
In love and compassion that's proven true.

The facade is cracking—no more alone…
Brief glimpses of a new safety zone.
"Please, Lord…Oh, would you please be gentle…
While penetrating this wounded soul?

"If the emotions and the feelings…
Come all at once…Lord, I'd be left reeling…
Rather, as the truth becomes clearer…
Please, my Father, draw me nearer…

"I want to be at peace…truly trust…
And Father, it's more than clear that I must.
Will you hold my hand? Oh, please, dear Lord?
It isn't easy to keep holding this sword…

"I give you my heart…Yes, even this place…
And as the tears run…I seek for your face…
Here I am, Lord…My heart is all yours…
Please come inside…and open these doors…"
—Sarah

chapter 13

What About Anger?

I was thinking a lot about James recently.

James was a little boy enrolled in the daycare where I worked in my late teens and early twenties. Very cute with his dark hair, dark eyes, and olive skin, he came to us through his foster mom.

His story was a sad one, and my heart immediately went out to him. He and his eight siblings had been found living in a van with their parents. Because of the circumstances, he was taken away from those he loved and placed in foster care. He was only five years old.

We were told very little about his situation other than his living conditions and that his father had a violent temper. His foster mom warned us that James gets angry at times and may need to be restrained so he doesn't hurt himself or the other children. She expressed concern about whether we had restraint training.

It made us all a little wary of him.

Things went well for a while, then one day another little boy grabbed a toy away from James and accidentally hit him on the arm.

The quiet, seemingly withdrawn little fellow flew into a rage unlike anything I had ever seen. The words that flew out of his mouth were enough to make all of us stare in slack-jawed amazement as James set out to take care of the offender. Feet and fists flying, he would have done significant damage if one of us hadn't intervened.

With his face contorted in rage, heavily accented curses spewed from his little mouth. A teacher's aide gazed at me in helplessness as I tried to separate James from the rest of the children.

Beside himself with anger, he picked up a little chair and flung it across the room. I motioned for the aide to take the other children outside, sighing in relief when they slipped away.

Now it was just James and me. Little as he was, I wasn't sure I could handle him. He scared me. His eyes, so dark and normal-looking before, flashed with hate. I did a little self-talk: *He is only five years old. I am much bigger and stronger than he is. I'm not afraid of him.*

Looking at me defiantly, he picked up a toy and threw it at the wall. CRASH!

"James," I said, speaking softly and trying to stay calm, "would you like to go outside?"

"NO!" he screamed. He cursed again, spitting at me like a wildcat.

The administrator stuck her head in the door. "If you need anything, I'm in the office," she said supportively. Everyone else had cleared out, either to the playroom or outside.

He reminded me of a wild animal. I thought of what his foster mother had told us, "He will be violent until he cries. If you can break through his anger and get him to cry, he will relax."

Hmmm... How can I make him cry?

I tried talking gently, but everything was met with a violent, "NO!" I tried distractions, getting out some of his favorite toys. It didn't work.

He sat hunkered down in the corner, glaring out of the corner of his eye.

I asked if I may hold him. "NO!" he replied. Once again words came out of his little mouth that made me blush.

I advanced on him, trying to break the stalemate by getting in his space, forcing him to look at me. I prepared to take some of his anger in fist form. Talking gently, I held a book in my hand. "I'm going to sit beside you and read this book," I said. Somehow I realized James needed love and a gentle touch.

When I sat down, he scooted as far from me as he could. I started to read and was pleased to see his anger fade as he became interested in the book. I slid closer, showing him the pages and talking gently to him.

Feeling pretty good about myself, I relaxed. Suddenly he spit at me. "Get away!" he screamed, striking out at me with his fists.

Okay, I decided, *it's time to put my restraint training to use.* I reached for him and carefully wrapped my arms around him, holding him firmly. He kicked and jerked wildly. I wrapped his legs in mine to keep him under control.

Spitting, cursing, and screaming, he writhed in anger and tried to bite me. Trying to avoid being bitten, I struggled to hold him without hurting him. He tried throwing his head back against my chest, aiming for my chin.

"James," I said soothingly as sweat broke out on my forehead, "I will let you go when you calm down and stop screaming. You cannot hit me." He swore so violently that his voice cracked under the strain.

I noticed my supervisor standing at the entrance to our room, observing in case I needed help. I wasn't sure how long I could hold on to him. His screams became hysterical.

Then all of a sudden something changed. Almost like a physical sensation, I felt it break.

James started to cry.

His little body shook and shuddered as he sobbed uncontrollably. I rocked

What About Anger?

him and sang, "Yes, Jesus loves me... Yes, Jesus loves me..." He continued crying and laid his sweaty head back against me. I finally felt him relax.

After a few more minutes of deep, heart-wrenching sobbing, his tears began to subside. I continued to sing as he sniffled. He nodded when I asked him if he was ready to go outside for fresh air. The angry, violent little boy had disappeared. The tears had washed it all away. As I rubbed his back and helped him with his shoes, he even had a smile for me.

My heart cried for the poor little fellow. For the grief that life had given him in his five short years. Hand in hand, we walked out to the playground.

Did I somehow, through that victory, magically establish a trust between me and him?

No.

Sad to say, we had to work through that explosive reaction many times. And sometimes I couldn't get James to relax. Sometimes his anger won. I could only imagine what he had seen in his life to make him so full of anger and hatred.

Sometimes I ended up with bruises on my legs and arms. Sometimes he spit in my face. He always cursed and swore in words no little boy should know. Sometimes, if he made a visible bruise, James and I would walk to the kitchen after the tears were over and he would put ice on my "hurty spots." He rarely said sorry, but he gently put on the ice for me.

Most of the teachers sighed when James arrived for the day. It was much more peaceful on the days he wasn't there.

But I loved him.

And I missed him when he didn't come. His dark brown eyes haunted me. The times when he smiled and let me hold him were so precious. I wondered if anyone else loved him. His foster mother was nice but very abrupt. There were no warm fuzzies there. His woundedness tore at my heart.

One day I came to work and James wasn't there. I got busy with the other children and soon asked a coworker, "Where's James?"

"Oh," she said, giving me a thumbs-up and a wink, "your life just got easier. James is gone. The state sent him to a new foster home. He left the area."

I tried to act nonchalant, but my heart reeled in surprise and grief. I had come to love the unpredictable boy. And now he was gone. Most likely I would never see him again. My coworkers were relieved, but I was devastated.

Even now I wonder… *Where is James today? What happened to him? Did he ever conquer his devastated emotions? Has anyone taken the time to love him? Did my prayers for him help?*

I see myself in James.

As I walked through the pain of facing my battles, I found myself dealing with feelings of anger that were almost as explosive as his. Of course, I didn't hit and scream, or spit and swear, but the way my heart raced and the irritation surged inside, I felt much like he did.

In my years of counseling with Mary, she encouraged me to show more of my emotions and to express some of the anger she thought was there. But I was way too controlled for that. It frustrated me when she told me that someday I would need to express my hidden anger, because I was determined never to allow that. I wasn't angry, and I wasn't about to express it. To me, anger showed a lack of self-control.

But as I walked through emotional healing years later, I faced anger that had been buried deep inside my heart. I felt anger that so much of my childhood was robbed because of choices I had made in my ignorance. Anger at choices others had made that caused me so much pain and fear. Anger that I struggled so much when others seemed to just glide along. Anger over things that still wounded and dominated me, but I had no control over. And sometimes an anger at God that scared me and shamed me.

During times of emotional stress, these angry feelings would surface quickly and take me off guard. When this happened, I often poured out my feelings on paper. Grabbing a pen, I wrote and wrote. Spewing through my fingers came emotions that had been buried deep inside.

Following is an example of me trying to process anger through my writing. This was after a troubling relationship created pain.

> **It is not the anger itself that is wrong. It is what we do with it that matters.**

I stand here tonight, and I'm okay.
Well, I thought I was. But I'm actually not. Inside me a volcano is erupting. Outside, I look okay.
Never before have I been so misunderstood.
Not when I was manhandled at work, because then I didn't speak. I didn't think I had a voice. I sucked it in and thought I was a loser who deserved it. Not when I became so thin that I wanted to die. Not even when I became so troubled I tried to die.
Why does this feel deeper? More disturbing than abuse?
Why do I feel so helplessly misunderstood?
I tried to walk carefully and wisely. I tried to speak to them. I listened to my husband and his words to wait.
Again and again I've questioned…agonized…prayed.
But now I am completely misunderstood. They won't hear me. And I can't do a thing about it. Deep inside me I hear/feel this "roar."
I am angry. I have to get this feeling out of my heart. I am so ashamed that I am angry. I'm crying my heart out at the injustice of seeking God and being misunderstood. Am I pitying myself? Maybe. Am I justified in my anger? Maybe that too.
But I don't like it. It isn't who God wants me to be.
Others may—but I may not.
"God…my God…I'm so sorry, Father. You know more than

anyone how I despise anger. Anger hurts. I want to give this all to you. All the tears, the restlessness within. The self-pity...the deep sadness...but most of all, this anger.

"It makes me want to lash out. But God...I want to be pure. Father, take this from me. I confess my anger...my self-pity.

"Place within me peace and acceptance. Give me beauty for these ashes...joy for this deep mourning...But most of all, Father, give me a pure heart. You have said, 'Vengeance is mine...' I must resign myself.

"Wash me whiter than snow. I'm all yours, Lord. All yours. Will you take my life and all my muck? My dirty, angry heart, and clean it? Then, God, use it for your glory."

This shows my struggle with anger. And the devastating guilt it produced.

I am thankful that God sent someone to walk with me. To help me learn that anger is a valid emotion. We can't just stuff it down and ignore it. And we don't want to. The feeling of anger is important because it often points to unresolved pain locked inside. God already knows that our anger is there—we can't hide it. It is not the anger itself that is wrong. It is what we do with it that matters. The Word says, "Be ye angry, and sin not: let not the sun go down upon your wrath" (Ephesians 4:26).

This Scripture clearly shows that although anger is an emotion created by God, we need to learn how to deal with it. Suppressed anger will erupt at some time and in some way. If it erupts in an uncontrolled way, it does unspeakable damage.

Look at all the ways anger has wounded people and hurt people. These wounded and hurting people then turn around and wound and hurt others. It's a vicious cycle.

The Bible warns us to deal with our anger immediately—don't even let the sun go down before dealing with it. Why? Because of the repercussions of suppressed anger.

In my own struggle, I needed to retrain my mind to examine my feelings and process them in a healthy way—not just pushing them away and feeling guilty for having them. Pushing them away never solves the problem.

"Jesus loves me this I know... For the Bible tells me so." It is such a little song—but it has a beautiful message. I sang it over and over to myself as I walked through each emotion. Many of them, it seemed, were locked in from my childhood and needed a childlike care to be healed. The song took me back to where these tangles started as a little girl and gave me so much peace. Little by little, as the box of emotions emptied, the pain of facing them became less.

We are all part of this fallen world; we all have emotions to deal with. Just as I have to deal with mine, so do you. Maybe you realize that you have allowed anger to fester and settle inside you. Maybe you have unspoken hurts that you refuse to think about. Maybe you have deep-down fears that control you—things that are causing bondage in your life.

Whatever it is, now is the time to face it. With God, you can do it. I encourage you to pull it out and look at it in all its ugliness. Then have a good cry over it. It doesn't matter how silly or childish it may feel, talk to God about it. Write it out if necessary, and then burn it to show that you have given it to God. Tell God how deeply it hurts, how angry you feel, how unfair it is, how confusing it is—and then lay it at His feet. He is the only One big enough to handle it.

God never meant for anger to manifest itself in the way it did for James. That poor little boy obviously had an angry father. I believe James was so wounded that he had no idea how to express anything but violent anger, and it was ruining his life.

I may never know what became of James, but I am thankful I had a chance to love him. Knowing him has helped me know my own heart.

"Thank you, God, for James. Bless him wherever he may be. If he is still fighting his emotions, show yourself to him in such a real way that he will find out what ultimate love feels like—love from YOU."

Mentor's Thoughts

As you follow the twisted threads of Sarah's journey, you may notice distinct phases she encountered. These are normal steps to healing from any kind of trauma.

Many of us have grieved after the death of a loved one. I have experienced that and know it is very real. But other kinds of trauma, such as suffering abuse, losing a relationship, or facing a shattered dream also require walking through grief.

Usually there is a loss of something—often something precious. It may be the loss of innocence because of abuse, or it may be simply the loss of the carefree life of a child because of how we responded to circumstances. Looking back, we see from an adult perspective that what seemed like the only safe way to deal with a difficult situation actually took something from us.

Facing this loss honestly, naming it for what it is, and then accepting the process to move toward healing is the only way to truly lay it to rest.

There are many phases or stages of emotions you may encounter as you walk through your journey of grief. Following are some of them:

> **Denial:** This usually happens early on when you refuse to look at the things that hurt you. Although your circumstances may not appear like such a big deal to others, the pain may be overwhelming. For an abused child, these things are too crushing to even think about. You cannot handle the emotions involved, so they are stuffed down and denied. But they don't disappear. Feelings of guilt, shame, fear, and loneliness become a part of you.[1]

---

[1] These steps, or stages, of grief were taken from various sources, with differing terminology. For those who wish to pursue this further, a good place to start is https://www.econdolence.com/learning-center/grief-and-coping/the-stages-of-grief.

Emotional crisis: When things come to a head and you don't want to deal with the festering pain anymore, you may feel like you are going crazy. A barrage of emotions may come pouring out of that locked-up area inside, throwing you into utter turmoil. Since you never allowed yourself to face intense emotions before, you do not know how to deal with them.

Thankfully, this is usually short-term, even though it will feel like a lifetime when you are dealing with it. It is best to have a trusted friend/mentor/counselor who understands what you are going through and can talk you through the turmoil.

Blaming: As you deal with all these flooding emotions and try to make sense of them, you might start the blame game. An endless series of "what ifs" go through your mind and you might blame yourself or others—or God.

You do need to honestly name any wrong that was done to you, but you cannot stop there. Placing blame can become a bondage in itself when you always blame others for your problems. If someone wronged you, you need to take it to your heavenly Father and then choose to forgive. If you cannot forgive, it holds you in bondage.

Forgiving does not mean the wrong someone did to you doesn't matter, it just says you are turning it over to God. This is the only way to find true healing and freedom. You must take those wrongs to the cross and release the hurt and the pain. Remember, that is what Jesus did with our sins.

If there is anything God shows you in your life that needs repentance and/or a change, take that to the cross too. Jesus is waiting with open arms to forgive you. He will take your load and show you how to walk in peace and freedom.

Anger: Feeling anger can be hard if you are a sensitive, caring person. When reality hits that a part of your life was lost to whatever pain you were dealing with, anger is the natural response. As hard as it is, this anger must be walked through in a healthy way to find true healing.

Anger is scary. It is unpredictable and causes hurt. For too many, anger in another person is what caused the emotional struggles in the first place. Since anger is so harmful, you may reason that it is never right to feel or show anger. But as you get to know the Father better, you will realize that even God can feel anger.

As you learn how to accept and deal with your emotions, anger will not be so scary. There is no sin in feeling anger because of what you have lost or what has been taken from you. The important thing is learning to give those feelings to God. This is not a onetime thing, but something we need to do daily…hourly…minute-by-minute.

Grief: As you accept your emotions and work through them, you need to grieve what you have lost. This requires admitting that something was lost, regardless of who was at fault. You may have lost the innocence of childhood, your trust in others, and many good memories. Of course, you will never be happy about your loss, but you can accept it and move on. The pain will always be there, but the intensity will pass. Accepting the grief requires feeling it. It may be necessary to allow yourself to cry—to sob out your deep pain. This may be the only way to truly release it.

Acceptance: It may take time to forgive or come to terms with the past. But slowly you can learn to accept this as a part of your history. You will be able to talk about your past without experiencing overwhelming feelings of rage, grief, or panic. Eventually you will be able to see the positive ways God has used what Satan meant for evil.

Depression: You may have acknowledged, accepted, moved on, but suddenly you face feelings of hopelessness, helplessness, and despair. This is because, even though you have taken many steps toward healing, the damage has not yet been repaired. Depression is a natural part of the grieving process. Just as hard physical work tires your muscles, so grieving exhausts the emotions. This often leads to depression, which detaches you emotionally from the hurtful situation. How long you are stuck here depends on how soon you realize you still have work to do and how willing you are to do what it takes.

> Your past is what it is. But your future will become what you allow God to make it.

Repairing the damage: This is the "renewing of your mind." You need to be honest with how your past caused you to react and respond in ways that were not healthy to your emotional well-being. For instance, a fear of rejection may have caused you to try to please others instead of being your true self. Or an inability to trust may have kept you from having close relationships. Or a misunderstanding of who God is may have given you a fear of opening your heart to the Spirit. Each of these reactions (and many more) will need to be identified as hurtful.

Once they are identified, deliberate steps need to be taken to change each reaction to a healthy one. This is not easy nor done quickly. New pathways need to be forged within your mind, and this takes time. I'm told it takes fifty repetitions to change a bad habit to a good one. It is crucial to saturate yourself with God's Word. This is the only Guide you can trust to renew your mind, since it was inspired by the One who created you. It will take time, and you may get impatient, but the healing is being done by the process. This is the hard work that will strengthen your mind.

Many people get stuck in one of these stages, but true freedom comes from walking faithfully with your Father. You will come to realize that even though the painful things in your past shaped who you became, so did every other life experience. Realizing you cannot change your past and then trusting everything to God—past, present, and future—will bring peace and rest to your soul.

You may experience these stages in a different order and to a greater or lesser degree. You may find yourself cycling back through previous stages or you might skip some entirely. Each person's journey is unique.

Your past is what it is. But your future will become what you allow God to make it.

Writing Out Your Thoughts...

1. What do you see in your past that was lost? Innocence? Peaceful childhood? Trust?

2. In what ways have you denied or downplayed the truth of your past?

3. What emotions are the most difficult for you to feel? What are the things that trigger those feelings?

4. Make two columns. On the right, list one or more things that have caused you pain in the past that you see were really not your fault. Ask God to help you forgive the people responsible for them.
   On the left, list the things that you are responsible for and need to deal with. Take the list to God and ask for His help.

5. How has someone else's anger hurt you in the past? Are you able to accept feelings of anger for wrongs done to you? How is anger scary to you?

6. How do the things you have lost affect you today?

7. What potential good can you see from negative events in the past? (Example: painful rejection taught me to be kind to others.)

> *And be renewed in the spirit of your mind; and that ye put on the new man, which after God is created in righteousness and true holiness.* Ephesians 4:23-24

chapter 14

Reactions

Most of us are aware of post-traumatic stress disorder in relation to war veterans. We think of PTSD as a mental health condition that happens only to those who have experienced the terror of being on the battlefield. But PTSD can also occur after other traumatic events.

Post-traumatic stress disorder is characterized by intrusive thoughts about the incident. There are flashbacks of distress or anxiety and an avoidance of similar situations. It manifests itself differently in different people.

A retired soldier may hear a vehicle backfire and immediately find himself flat on the ground in the position of defense—his heart pounding, sweat pouring, and his body shaking violently. The noise triggered a reaction in him. Even though he is no longer at war, he is dealing with post-traumatic stress.

Someone who has recently been in a car accident may hear a door slam and immediately smell smoke and hear sirens.

PTSD can be triggered by certain situations or even certain smells that mimic a time you found traumatic. Maybe a doctor's visit that was extremely painful will trigger feelings of panic the next time you step into the doctor's office. Any reminder of past threatening events or interactions can bring it on.

My journey through healing triggered emotional PTSD in ways for which I wasn't prepared. It took me right back to the hopeless, helpless feeling of being anorexic and full of shame and fear. It felt like I was right there again, facing emotions I had hidden since childhood.

These times were really scary, but I share them so you can recognize them. And above all, so you can find comfort in knowing there is a way through them.

I'd like to share a first-hand experience of PTSD triggered by needing to fight through a reaction that mimicked a time of rejection.

> It's happening again…
>
> My heart is racing. What is happening? Hands and fingers numb, my mind tries to catch up with my body.
>
> Air…I need air…Get me outside! I need to breathe…Desperate prayers fill my mind as I try to understand what is going on. I should be safe. There is nothing here that can harm me. But my body says it's not safe. My heart also says it's not okay, and my emotions say, "No, no, no, no, no, no…!"
>
> I feel an erratic hammering at my subconscious until I break, and the tears come. With a ferocity driven by the evil one, my mind searches for the source, the reason for this reaction. My thoughts come in waves. I have no way of deciphering what is reality and what is "pit thinking."
>
> Why can't I deal with these feelings? I've had feelings all my life. What is so different now?
>
> It is because my walls are gone. My protection lies in only One venue. I have no guards. No outlets. No self-protection. Nothing.
>
> I am broken.

He's been working on me, and sometimes it is more painful than I can express—yet it is heartbreakingly beautiful.

Empty-handed, tears racing down my cheeks, I stand before Him.

Head bowed in shame, I weep with confusion and self-hatred, shaking and trembling. I feel covered in shame and humiliation, reeking with doubts and confusion.

> If you find yourself facing scary reactions as you walk back through your emotions, allow yourself to feel them, as difficult as they may be.

"God..." I wail. "I don't know what to do about this. I feel like a mess."

He gives me an inner vision. Tenderly, ever so gently, He reaches for my chin. I sense Him nearing and flinch. Is He upset at me? I'm such a mess. He slowly tips my chin up and waits. He waits until my eyes meet His.

"Come to me. You are mine."

Struck, almost frightened, by the love in His gaze, I notice that I cannot see my shame anymore.

I step back from Him, fighting doubts and fears. When His tender touch leaves my chin, I start shaking and trembling again. The shame returns.

"God!" I cry out in fear. "I need you."

"Trust me. Come to me." His voice is like the sound of many waters...beautiful and sweet.

I realize with sudden clarity that this is all I need. If I am connected to Him, He will take my woundedness. It is not mine to carry.

It is His.

I need only to stay within His touch. Sheltered in His arms.

If you find yourself facing scary reactions as you walk back through your emotions, allow yourself to feel them, as difficult as they may be.

Reactions

Ask God to help you understand His perfect love, His acceptance, and His care for you. The light of His love shining into you can turn your ugliest scar into something beautiful.

God never works on us just for our own good. If we stay connected to Him, He will show us how to use the beauty of brokenness to show others a better way.

Mentor's Thoughts

Sarah did an excellent job in describing a very difficult part of her journey. Facing these emotional reactions is a normal part of healing from trauma, and it can be helpful to know that others also face them.

The cause of many of these reactions to childhood trauma is summed up in one of Sarah's sentences: "Facing emotions I had hidden since childhood…"

Locking down feelings that are too much to handle does not make them disappear. They are still there and need to be faced to find true healing and peace. Sarah speaks of walls being gone. These are the walls in her mind that hid her traumatic memories.

She also uses the term "self-protection." It is difficult to lay down the methods and props we normally use to protect ourselves from harm or bad feelings. Placing our trust in Jesus Christ is not easy when trust has been broken at a young age.

It often helps to understand what is going on—to know that there is an actual physical reason for something that feels so out of control. PTSD is triggered by trauma that results in faulty processing and storing of distressing memories.

God has created our brains with an alarm system to keep us safe. The amygdala is a small, almond-shaped part of our brain that plays a big role in this. It helps us regulate our emotions, especially fear, and helps us evaluate if something is a threat. It also helps us form and store emotional memories and to predict where danger may come from in the future.

Another area of the brain, the prefrontal cortex, helps us think through our decisions, enabling us to put on the "brakes" when we realize something we feared is not a threat after all. It helps us regulate the emotional responses triggered by the amygdala.

> God's message of hope in this is that He can meet us in our pain and trauma and lead us through it.

A simple explanation of PTSD is that our alarm system overreacts and our braking system fails. In a person with PTSD, the alarm system is overly sensitive and triggers easily, while the part responsible for logical thinking and memory is not working properly. It's a bit like stepping on the accelerator in your car when you don't really need to and then finding out you have no brakes.[1]

In Sarah's story, we see how her repressed emotions from her childhood years caused an overreaction in her alarm system. This first triggered a physical response—to get to safety—followed by an emotional reaction that flooded her with negative feelings. You see the logical part trying to put on the brakes with the quiet voice of truth that this is not a dangerous situation. It is okay.

In the end, we see Sarah coming to Jesus for healing, letting

---

[1] For more on PTSD, several good books are *The Body Keeps the Score* by Bessel van der Kolk and *The PTSD Workbook: Simple, Effective Techniques for Overcoming Traumatic Stress Symptoms* by Mary Beth Williams and Soili Poijula. See additional resources in the back of this book. You may also want to look up these online sites: https://www.verywellmind.com/what-exactly-does-ptsd-do-to-the-brain-2797210 and https://www.brainline.org/article/how-ptsd-affects-brain.

Him put on the brakes and holding her until the storm subsided.

God's message of hope in this is that He can meet us in our pain and trauma and lead us through it. It may be a difficult journey, but it is worth the hard work to find rest. This all starts with the renewing of the mind we read of in Romans 12:2.

Learning to trust the Father is very important. Without this trust, we cannot run to Him in times of distress. The following illustration of learning to TRUST can help us in times of fearful reactions.

T = Talk to your fears. Tell them they cannot control you.

R = Remind yourself that your Father is bigger than your fears and has already conquered them.

U = Understand God's heart for you through knowing His Word.

S = Slow down and purposefully think through what scares you. Speak what you know to be true.

T = Turn it over to God; He can deal with any situation much better than you can. TRUST that He will work it out for your good and His glory.

Writing Out Your Thoughts...

1. Think of things that scare you. Do you remember when you first started being afraid?

2. Tell of a time or times when you felt the way Sarah described—heart pounding, unable to breathe, panic.

3. Do you feel you can trust God to protect you when you feel afraid? Why or why not?

4. Can you think of any way or ways God might be able to use your painful memories to do good today?

> *Behold, I stand at the door, and knock: if any man hear my voice, and open the door, I will come in to him, and will sup with him, and he with me. To him that overcometh will I grant to sit with me in my throne, even as I also overcame, and am set down with my Father in his throne.* Revelation 3:20-21

Part Five
Under God's Control

As we give to God what was never ours in the first place, the fear and confusion inside our heart and mind is replaced by peace and freedom. Satan tells us that freedom is making our own choices—in not letting anyone tell us what to do. But true freedom comes only when we choose to surrender to God. After all, He created us.

In Part Five, Sarah discovers the freedom of God's upside-down kingdom. She learns that this freedom comes in daily choices to obey—even when it feels scary. She realizes that God can be trusted no matter what. For the first time, her heart finds peace and rest in letting Him take control.

Chapter 15

Swapping My Bondage

Emotional healing takes time and patience. As an energetic, impatient person by nature, this wore me out.

As desperately as I wanted to find freedom, I sometimes failed to recognize my bondage. And that can easily happen. Unless bondage comes to the light of God's truth, it might not feel like bondage. It might just feel normal.

I had never dreamed that healing would come at such a cost—or with so much turmoil. I'm not saying I regret this journey. Not at all. Though it felt messy and painful at times, it brought me to the feet of my Father more than ever before.

A friend recently told me about a woman who spent years on narcotics for pain. When she realized what these narcotics were doing to her body, she asked the doctors if she could get off them. They told her it was impossible—that her body had become so dependent on these addictive drugs that going off them quickly would kill her. But she was determined to conquer them, so against doctors' recommendations, she started slowly backing off on the meds.

What happened to her body was so intense that she became dreadfully ill. She actually thought she might die. Shaking and vomiting, she saw hallucinations and her skin crawled. But she persisted until she was finally free of the meds, and her body settled down.

But she still had a problem—her pain. Which was why she had taken the narcotics in the first place.

She now takes marijuana for her pain, but she doesn't see that her bondage has just changed faces. To her, taking marijuana instead of ten different narcotics seems better. And in some ways, it is.

But is she really free?

Not entirely. She is still in bondage to a drug. Marijuana is addictive and will probably control her.

> The root is learning to give up control—again and again—to the only One who is qualified to control my life.

I found myself in the exact same place, although in a different way.

As I went back through the emotions that triggered the eating disorder in the first place, I faced a barrage of sensations. It was ugly, and my emotions made no sense. I reacted in tears and deep sadness to the slightest things, pushing against those I loved most.

Instead of recognizing what was going on, I was overwhelmed by how I felt. My out-of-control emotions made me angry, and a sense of despondency settled on me. It seemed hopeless that I would ever change.

The different emotions were all linked. Withdrawing from a lifetime of disordered thinking patterns and habits brought withdrawal symptoms as real as for a person getting off drugs. Without my usual pathways, my ways of coping, I found myself floundering.

As my mind and my habits were forced to find new pathways, a feeling of helplessness triggered a soul-searching beyond anything I had ever faced before.

It was hard to let my old habits go—they were all I had ever known. My eating disorder was a way of control in my life. It gave me a sense of empowerment. It was something I could do right. Losing it felt like losing a part of who I was.

As I struggled to let go, I felt God showing me a very real concern: *I must be careful not to just swap one form of bondage for another.*

As we forge new pathways in our brain, we must be vigilant. What may look like freedom may actually be a form of bondage with a new face. Each emotion and each new habit must be examined and evaluated in the light of God's Word. Then, with God's help, we can retrain our thinking processes in healthy ways. It takes patience and perseverance. And we cannot walk alone.

The root is learning to give up control—again and again—to the only One who is qualified to control my life.

I need to stop and ask repeatedly, "What is the proper response to this emotion?"

I need to drop everything I think I know and focus on the bottom line: "God, fix these wounded thought processes. Help me properly manage these feelings."

And then—and only then—can I open my heart and let the Lord show me how I can be victorious.

In Him.

Mentor's Thoughts

Our poor dog never seemed to relax. Jack was a beagle/pug mixture with lots of energy. When tied to the doghouse, he would pull on his collar until he coughed and choked. We finally got him a

Swapping My Bondage

harness, but he pulled at that until he wore the cable through. Then he was off and running. In desperation, we put him in the meadow with the horses. Surely the woven wire fence would hold him.

But Jack didn't like it. He trotted the perimeter of the fence, searching for a place to get out. He tried digging under the fence, first in one spot and then in another. When we closed up one potential escape route, he immediately started on another. His whole being longed to be out and running for the horizon. We finally sold Jack because he was just too much dog for our young children.

I often wonder if Jack ever learned to be content in captivity. If only he could have seen our meadow as a safe place with plenty of space to run. I see my unbroken self as much like that dog. It is hard to accept the safe confines of godly living and be content where He places us.

When I started this journey of accountability with Sarah, God pointed out my own unhealthy eating habits. I knew if I expected Sarah to listen to my advice on healthy living, then I must choose this pathway myself. Just as Sarah had to learn to have a healthy attitude about food, so did I.

The question came down to, "What do I want?" I knew I wanted to be healthy and to live a full, active life. I also wanted to care for my body because it is the temple of the Holy Spirit. The problem was, my immediate comfort kept getting in the way.

Maybe we could see it in a "big picture" versus "little picture" perspective. In Genesis 25, we read how Esau gave up his birthright (big picture) to appease his hunger (little picture). In the book of Judges we read of Samson, a man of great strength whom God raised up to do His work. But Samson was held captive by his physical appetites. He insisted on having the heathen women he wanted (little picture), which led to his downfall and seriously hampered his ability to carry out the work God had intended for him (big picture).

It was the same for me. I needed to decide what I wanted and then accept the pathway it required.

Choosing this pathway often means surrendering SELF. It means making difficult choices and giving up some things we really want. We can find ourselves going around and around, just like our dog, Jack—always looking for a way out of "captivity." But when this happens, the main problem is not the fences in our lives but our attitude toward them.

God has been changing my understanding of what His fences represent. I need to see it as His protection from my SELF. Out there are dangers; inside is the protection of living the way I have been created to live. I need to be thankful for the fences my Father places in my life and see them through His eyes for what they really are—safety.

> Giving our all to God is a lifelong journey. We do it one step at a time, one surrender at a time, one day at a time.

No matter what bondage, disorder, or captivity we find ourselves in, we need to take an honest look at our attitude about the fences in our lives. True freedom is not having no boundaries. Just as being free to drive on the highway requires following certain laws, so true freedom is accepting the safe boundaries put in place by the One who created us.

As the Father calls us to walk close to His heart, He will show us

Swapping My Bondage

anything that comes in the way of giving our all to Him. Perhaps the most difficult of all the idols we must give up is the idol of control—of doing things *my* way instead of God's way.

Giving our all to God is a lifelong journey. We do it one step at a time, one surrender at a time, one day at a time.

Writing Out Your Thoughts...

1. What boundaries has God placed in your life that feel like captivity? Parents' rules? Church rules? Things you read in the Bible?

2. Do you ever feel a restlessness or discontent inside? What do you think may cause this feeling? Describe a time you felt this.

3. Read Matthew 16:24-26. What do you think it means to lose your life to find it? Is there anything in your life that may be hindering your walk with God?

4. What habits do you know you should change, but you struggle to let them go?

> *Then said Jesus unto his disciples, If any man will come after me, let him deny himself, and take up his cross, and follow me.* Matthew 16:24

chapter 16

Sorting It Out

But it doesn't make sense. I don't understand.

I looked again at the number on the scale. It seemed okay. But then I looked at my body and saw something else—fat. It was not okay. Which should I believe? By now I had learned that I couldn't trust my feelings. *I must go by fact. I have to trust the scale.*

I had worked so hard to lose my extra weight. I had clamped down tightly, eating just enough to keep going. Day after day, I had concentrated on eating healthy foods—salads, good carbs, good fats, and lots of protein. I had tried my best to learn how much to eat and what was good for me. It hadn't been easy.

Slowly but surely I had begun to rewire some of those areas of stunted growth in my brain. I had finally gotten to the place where I could hesitantly weigh myself—but I still almost always reacted negatively and wondered if the scale was deceiving me.

With my husband and Hannah providing me with accountability, I had agreed to a certain number where I should maintain my weight—no lower. But when I hit my goal, I wanted to keep losing weight. I had a very real fear of gaining weight again. And I still felt fat! But I realized that in my own eyes I may always seem overweight.

Hannah had explained that food in itself is not bad and had been trying to get me to reintroduce some new foods into my diet. It was hard for me to wrap my mind around the idea that it wasn't food that made me anorexic or bulimic—or overweight. It was the mishandling of it.

It was all so new. Could I really eat some chocolate? Part of a fry pie? Real fruit popsicles? A French fry or two? A small slice of pizza? *No way. I can't do that.*

But I did. Forcing myself to believe the truth, I ate some "taboo" foods that my mind had always told me were bad and must either be cut out or purged. And now the scale wasn't moving! It made me leery of it. *I can't eat these foods and be okay, can I?* It was baffling. My head was a mess.

It put me into an emotional spin. One minute I was crying and the next I was full of joy. The swing of emotions made it difficult to see if I was making any progress. But it felt like a new and deeper area I hadn't seen before.

Is this healing?

> It wasn't food that made me anorexic or bulimic—or overweight. It was the mishandling of it.

I realized that my fears were more deeply rooted than I had thought. Always before, whenever I had eaten any of these foods, it was with shame or because I had to. I had never really enjoyed them. They always came with a price: a session in the bathroom eliminating any trace of their existence.

But now, little by little, one bite at a time, I was stepping into territory that was totally unfamiliar. It created a frustrated feeling in me. My head wanted to shout out all the ways this was wrong, spouting all the eating disorder lies I had told myself most of my life.

At the same time, I felt a sense of awe—a pull to keep going. I heard the voices of truth breaking through the noise.

Is this something I can actually do? Is this what healing looks like? It brought confusion, and yet I sensed I was on the right way.

It was exhilarating!

Mentor's Thoughts

"What is healing?"

Ask this question to a former alcoholic or drug addict, and they may say it is never done—it comes one day at a time, one step at a time, one minute at a time. They know that even if they are living clean, there will always be a weak spot they need to remain aware of.

Anytime we allow Satan to ensnare us in bondage, it will become a weak spot in our armor. Since I was never an alcoholic or addicted to drugs, I am less likely to fall into that temptation. However, since I have indulged in gluttony and my health suffered because of it, I must remain aware that I could easily fall back into that snare if I am not careful.

What do we imagine life is like for someone "healed" from an eating disorder or other form of bondage? The answer may depend on our choice of lenses through which we view life. If our life is centered in Christ, and our heart, mind, and soul is steeped in His Word, then every thought, word, and action will be filtered through the Spirit of Truth Jesus spoke of: "Howbeit when he, the Spirit of truth, is come, he will guide you into all truth" (John 16:13).

Truth always lines up with God's Word. Satan is the father of deception and is very subtle in trying to deceive us. He rarely uses obvious lies, instead putting questions into our mind. Even if we know we are living and eating healthily, he will bring questions that throw suspicion on concrete facts. Even if the scale says we are okay, he will bring in questions and cause confusion.

This causes disordered thinking, which is defined as "not functioning in a healthy way." Seeing ourselves as fat when we are skeletally thin is definitely the result of a mind that is not healthy.

Healthy thinking requires making choices that may not "feel" right. It requires learning that facts come before feelings. We must choose to believe the truth regardless of our feelings.

> True strength lies not in forbidding ourselves of all pleasures but in accepting the gifts of God with thanksgiving and moderation.

All-or-nothing thinking also falls into the "disordered" category, as everything is viewed as either good or bad, with no center line. This may be true for some things, but usually that is not the case. Food, for instance, is a gift from God to nourish our bodies. Is any food absolutely bad? Yes, if we have a severe allergy to peanuts, then peanuts are absolutely bad for us. But in general, it is not the food that is bad—it is how we use it.

Learning about nutrition is an important step in understanding how and what to eat. We always come back to moderation. We must learn which foods are nutritious enough to eat a lot of and which ones should be eaten only occasionally. But we should understand that we can eat anything in moderation. Paul says in 1 Corinthians 6:12, "All things are lawful unto me, but all things are not expedient: all things are lawful for me, but I will not be brought under the power of any."

Not being "brought under the power of" goes two ways. We will not give in to our cravings and eat too many fattening and unhealthy foods, and we also will not be brought under the power of delusions that say we must totally abstain from certain foods. True strength lies not in forbidding ourselves of all pleasures but in accepting the gifts of God with thanksgiving and moderation.

So what is healing? It is learning the difference between Satan's bondage and God's gifts. It is learning to know the still, small voice of the Shepherd—and to follow that voice until it drowns out any other voices that would lead us into untruth. It also means that truth always comes before feelings.

It begins with the ultimate Truth—God's Word hidden in our hearts.

Writing Out Your Thoughts...

1. What feelings have been keeping you from believing facts? Do you *feel* fat? Or maybe you *see* fat on yourself even when others say you are thin? What doubts and fears do you feel even though others tell you they are not true?

2. What things do you see as all bad or all good? Is there any food you are being told is okay but you have trouble accepting? Write out what "center line" thinking might look like and how you can believe it is okay to eat this food.

3. What are other negative things you believe about yourself? Does the voice inside tell you how ugly and stupid you are—that you are a loser and no one really likes you? Now find a Bible verse that tells how God views you and speak back against that lie with God's own truth.

4. Maybe you want to live free of the inner tyrant, but you are afraid to let go of certain things. What are your fears?

> *I am the good shepherd, and know my sheep, and am known of mine…My sheep hear my voice, and I know them, and they follow me.* John 10:14, 27

chapter 17

Backwards Freedom

We all want freedom, right? We want freedom to make our own choices, freedom to serve God, freedom to worship where and when we want, and freedom to do the things we are convicted to do.

But what really is freedom?

We often think of freedom in terms of being free from restrictions. Unbound. Loosed and let go. My dictionary has about fifteen different definitions. What struck me as I read each one is that freedom comes at a cost.

A sure way to truly recognize freedom is when we have been in bondage.

We see that analogy played out perfectly when a captive dog is finally unrestrained. The exuberance with which it runs and bounds is the exact opposite of being tied. The dog recognizes freedom because it had previously been bound.

Many lives have been lost to purchase a country's freedom, and many a parental heart sacrificed to allow a child freedom of choice. A prisoner recognizes freedom because he has been confined to a jail cell.

Jesus paid the ultimate price for freedom, the highest price imaginable—His life.

But freedom doesn't always come the way we expect it. And often it comes at such a high price that we cannot pay for it on our own.

Sometimes freedom comes through tears, pain, and heartache. And sometimes what looks like bondage is actually freedom in the kingdom of God.

To me, it seems like "backwards freedom."

Maybe your work goes unnoticed and you see someone else taking the credit for it. Where's the freedom in that? Could it be that God is allowing it so you are freed from the bondage of pride or self-righteousness?

> Backwards freedom is real freedom. It is God's way.

Or maybe your good intentions become misunderstood and suddenly your reputation is at stake. How can that equal freedom? Is it possible that because of it God is drawing you closer to Him and freeing you from the chains of people pleasing?

Or maybe it's something you've surrendered time and again. You've given it up over and over, but it keeps holding you fast, tempting to destroy you. With purity of heart, you fight the talons of evil and conquer for a time, only to find that you are off course in another area. That's the cruelest of bondage, right?

Or could it be freedom in a different sense?

What if God, who knows your heart better than you do yourself, is trying your faith? What if the trial of your faith causes you to become more patient, more godly, more useful to Him? Isn't that freedom?

What if the very thing you find so binding is the only way to true freedom?

Consider the drunkard or drug addict. He is bound by alcohol or drugs. You could completely take it from him, never let him get near another drug or alcoholic beverage, and watch him closely every day. But is that freedom?

No, because unless he can face a drug offer or a beer, and by the grace and strength of God turn away, he is not totally free. It will continue to haunt him, and on the down days he will succumb to temptation.

The only way he will ever be really free is through a lot of heartache, pain, and tears—which will look like a lot more torment. But out of that incredible fight will come a freedom beyond anything he imagined—the power to be in control of his choices.

To the sexually abused, freedom means looking into the shame and the pain and facing it head-on. Yes, acceptance and admittance can bring back the trauma, and revisiting it may cause unwanted reactions. It will be a dark, gloomy pathway—one laced with tears and anger and surrounded by shadows and shame. It doesn't look like freedom at all. It looks like death. And to walk it feels like death.

But out of the midst of the tears and surrender comes a person at peace. A person willing to forgive the abuser. A person whose dignity and self-confidence are restored by the grace of God. That is true freedom.

Think about my battle with anorexia. I was completely bound and controlled by the avoidance of food and the number on the scale. They could have force-fed me in a clinical environment. They could have demanded that I get rid of the scale. They could have watched me with hawk eyes and surrounded me with rules and plans.

But would I have been free?

No.

Unless I fight the demon that causes this disorder, choosing to eat on my own and turning away from lying and deception, I cannot have total freedom.

Gaining freedom will mean a battle for your life—a total surrender of your ideas and plans. It will mean a complete mind renewal, a messy process that may feel like punishment.

It doesn't look like freedom at all.

But out of that fight will come beautiful freedom—freedom beyond anything you can attain in any other way. It is freedom to live exuberantly with no secrets. Freedom to enjoy life and to trust others. Freedom to allow others to walk with you and not hide behind a wall of shame. Freedom to eat and not be ashamed. Freedom to exercise and enjoy it. Freedom to accept your body and your mind.

It is freedom to choose life—not death.

But what if this freedom comes through tears and heartache? What if it is God's mercy that things do not go the way we planned?

Whether in this life or the next, we will someday be completely free—but on God's terms and conditions. He wants our open arms of surrender. God leads the way, and we trust Him.

Backwards freedom is real freedom. It is God's way.

Mentor's Thoughts

The "backwards freedom" Sarah wrote of is one of the paradoxes of the Christian life. It requires going the opposite way our human, fleshly heart wants to go.

The paradoxes in Christian living include many things: giving up our life to gain life, having nothing but possessing all things, finding strength in weakness, and giving up our will to find freedom. To live as a Christ follower, we must fight our natural inclinations and trust in the upside-down way of God's kingdom.

Paul describes some of these paradoxes in 2 Corinthians 6:8-10: "By honour and dishonour, by evil report and good report: as deceivers, and yet true; as unknown, and yet well known; as dying, and, behold, we live; as chastened, and not killed; as sorrowful, yet alway rejoicing; as poor, yet making many rich; as having nothing, and yet possessing all things."

When my children were small, the house got rather noisy at times. The noisier the children got, the louder I raised my voice. How else could I expect them to hear me? My quiet husband gave me a loving suggestion that maybe if I talked more quietly, they would also be quieter. I was skeptical, but I decided to try it since volume was not working.

The next time conflict broke out and the noise level escalated, instead of raising my voice, I lowered it and spoke softly. For a time, no one noticed or paid me any heed. But about the time I was feeling rather smug and thinking how I would inform my husband of his failed advice, one of the children noticed my quiet attempts at communicating. Quickly she hushed the others with, "Quiet! Mom's trying to talk!" I continued speaking softly until they had quieted enough to hear me. There were some sheepish looks as they realized how loud they had been compared to my quiet admonition.

I would like to say I never raised my voice again, but that would not even be close to the truth. However, I learned an important lesson that day. God's Word tells us in Proverbs 15:1, "A soft answer turneth away wrath: but grievous words stir up anger." There it was—another paradox of God's way. Instead of matching shouting with shouting, do it God's way and answer anger and volume with kind,

> What looks scary, ugly, or painful to me may actually be something that ultimately brings peace, beauty, strength, and joy.

Backwards Freedom

quiet dignity. It usually works.

It comes down to being able to understand that we only see a small part of the picture, but God sees the whole thing. What looks scary, ugly, or painful to me may actually be something that ultimately brings peace, beauty, strength, and joy. The test comes in learning to trust my Father and to believe He is working all things for my good and His glory.

That is true freedom.

Paradox

The world's way says do not bow,
I need my way; I want it now.

Our dignity demands our rights;
Do not give up without a fight.

The kingdom way seems upside down—
Give it all up to gain a crown?

The things I keep, that's what I'll lose.
My way—or God's? I get to choose.

Seeking for peace, I hear His call…
I give it up and gain it all.

—Hannah

Writing Out Your Thoughts...

1. What is something (or things) you want, but you know it is best for you not to have? Why not?

2. What comes to mind when you think of the term "giving up"? In your own words, how would you explain the difference between giving up and giving over?

3. One paradox of Christian living is that we humble ourselves to be exalted. Too often we mistake humility for being humiliated. What is the difference between humbling yourself and degrading yourself?

4. In what ways can you humble yourself before an almighty God without feeling shame? What does God's Word say about how God feels about you? (See Jeremiah 29:11 and John 3:16.)

> *And we know that all things work together for good to them that love God, to them who are the called according to his purpose.* Romans 8:28

chapter 18

A New Gauge

The old school van was truly a relic. One by one this fell off, that stopped working, and something else dragged. But it still ran, and if we took it to the right place it even passed inspection. I didn't mind its rattles and idiosyncrasies.

Until one day.

It was my week to drive the school children, and there seemed to be a slight problem with this beast of a van. My husband had checked it out and wasn't overly concerned. "Somehow some water must have sloshed out of the radiator," he said. "I filled it again." Whatever it was, clouds of steam were now billowing from under the hood.

It had steamed some on the way to school on the morning run, but I ignored it. That afternoon, as I headed toward school to pick up the scholars, the steam got worse and worse. Soon the inside of the van was steaming up, and I was sure the whole thing could blow up or burst into flames.

I pulled off the road and shut off the engine. *Now what?* I was relieved when a man from church stopped and asked if I needed help. "Yes! Thank you!" I was so glad to let him peer under the hood to check things out.

The radiator was dry.

So that was the problem. "Didn't the gauge show that the engine was hot?" my rescuing angel asked.

"Well, no."

You see, the gauges didn't work. It was just another endearing characteristic of this relic. Things had to get really bad before we could tell there was a problem. I was so thankful I had pulled off the road before I ruined something for good.

> No enemy of the soul can mess with the gauges God intended to work for your benefit unless you allow him to.

I started imagining what it would be like to drive a new vehicle to take the children to school. Would I know how to read the gauges? Would I trust them? Or would I ignore them because I had learned to live without them? If the "check engine" light came on and the gauge showed that the engine was getting a little hot, would I just keep going?

Or would I trust the gauge?

This is what I am learning to do on my healing journey.

My gauge had been broken. It was my own fault, because I'm the one who disabled it with one bad choice after another. Every time the gauge started showing the slightest bit of hunger, I shut it down because I was afraid it would make me lose control. With my anorexia, I learned to switch the feeling of hunger into a feeling of power, allowing me to ignore it. As the pangs of hunger wracked my system, I shut the gauge down again and again. I saw hunger as a pathetic weakness.

I did the same while I was bulimic. I never allowed hunger to send its pangs to my brain. I doused it with bingeing and purging, deadening it in every way possible.

Just like the gauges in the old school van, the hunger gauge in my body didn't work anymore. It had been effectively disabled because the "do-it-yourselfer" in me insisted that obeying it would ruin my engine.

But that was back then.

Now I am being made new. God has opened my eyes in a new way toward this body I have been blessed to live in. My vehicle is a special edition classic designed just for me by the Master Mechanic. He knows what is best for this vehicle because it is actually His. It always was. I am just loaning it for now—and I'm accountable for it in every way.

Recently I became aware that the gauge is working again. I felt a twinge of hunger for the first time in years, and it stopped me in my tracks. My first response was annoyance, followed by shame, but the long struggle to pull my mind out of the ruts of my eating disorder has started to pay off. A still small voice whispered, "It's okay. This is not a bad feeling. This is okay."

Before, hunger was a sign of danger, of weakness. A sign that I was headed in the wrong direction. Something I couldn't allow in my life.

But now my mind is no longer controlled by an eating disorder. My gauge is working for my benefit. With the hope of Christ in me, I will order all those condemning "do-it-yourself" thoughts out of my mind. I have a choice. Today I will choose life.

I will accept the Master Mechanic's gauges, created to make my body work beautifully for me—and for Him.

Join me, dear struggling friend. Let's set our gauges to the factory setting. This gauge is pointed to life, hope, and peace—through Jesus Christ. If He did it for me, He can do it for you. No matter where you are, there is HOPE.

No enemy of the soul can mess with the gauges God intended to work for your benefit unless you allow him to.

Choose life.

A New Gauge

Mentor's Thoughts

Have you ever had a phone or another electronic device reset to factory settings? I have. After setting up my phone as I wanted it, for some reason one day it reverted to factory settings. Changing the settings had taken time and effort, so losing all my preferences was an annoyance. However, I realized that whatever had caused my phone to reset was actually a safety feature put into it by the manufacturer to bring it back to the original settings. Otherwise the phone might have stopped working.

Our body also has factory settings. We are born with certain settings in our brain and body that sense and report things like heat, cold, pain, and hunger. These are special safety features designed to protect us.

Maybe it's a little like our John Deere lawn tractor. There was a safety feature under the seat. When enough weight was on the seat to push a switch, the motor ran just fine. But if there was not enough weight to activate the switch, the motor would not run. For the safety of the operator, this protective feature installed by the manufacturer was an excellent idea.

However, it became a nuisance when the motor died every time we wanted to jump off quickly to pick up something or open a gate. Also, we thought our children were old enough to run the mower safely before they were heavy enough to activate the switch. So you guessed it... We disabled the switch. Now the tractor's engine ran even if no one was on the seat. It was what we wanted. But without the factory setting, we needed to use extra caution.

In the same way, it is possible to change the factory settings in our body that God put in place as safety features. For instance, the feeling of hunger is a complex interaction between the digestive system, the endocrine system, and the brain. When our body signals the need for more nutrition, blood sugar and insulin levels drop. This causes our gut to produce a hormone called ghrelin. Ghrelin travels to the brain and releases the hormone Neuropeptide Y, which stimulates our appetite. This is how our body was created to work.

When we ignore or misread these signals, we actually rewire our brain to respond differently. In people with anorexia and bulimia, signals from other parts of the brain override those sent from the area that regulates appetite. These signals can come from fear or other strong emotions.

If we shut down hunger signals when our body is calling out for nutrition, we run the risk of starving ourselves, ruining our health, and destroying our ability to think clearly. On the other hand, if we use feelings of hunger to indulge in fattening, unhealthy foods, we will develop an addiction to sugar and may become unable to differentiate between signals for hunger and cravings for sugar.

Messing with the factory settings of our body causes an inability to read and understand the "gauges," or signals, our body sends. So how do we get back to factory settings? If we have shut down hunger signals and no longer feel or trust them, we may have to relearn how to use them.

We must learn to listen to our body and trust the signals it is sending. We must pay attention to what we are eating and how much, then take notice of how we feel half an hour...an hour...or two hours after a meal. If we don't feel full until half an hour after a meal, we keep that in mind and stop eating before we feel full. Going through this learning process will be much easier with a coach or mentor to guide us.

Before long we will gain confidence in the signals our body is sending and learn to eat the right amount. We will also gain confidence that the One who created us has designed our system perfectly and will show us how to get peak performance from our body.

After all, we are not our own. We are temples for God's Holy Spirit.

Writing Out Your Thoughts...

1. How does hunger make you feel? Are you ever ashamed or angry to feel hunger? What do you do when you feel hungry?

2. Is there anything about your body that you feel you must control? Tell what and why you feel this way.

3. Is being careful not to overeat or not to eat too much junk food the same as totally restricting certain foods? Why or why not?

4. Explain the difference between totally restricting a food and eating it in moderation.

5. What foods do you not allow in your diet? If you could be convinced they are safe, what foods would you really like to eat?

What? know ye not that your body is the temple of the Holy Ghost which is in you, which ye have of God, and ye are not your own? For ye are bought with a price: therefore glorify God in your body, and in your spirit, which are God's. 1 Corinthians 6:19-20

chapter 19

Try It MY Way

I like to do things my way. To follow a certain routine.

I get up in the morning, have my quiet time with Jesus, drink a cup of warm lemon water, get my coffee, and then step outside to listen to the birds and breathe the fresh air.

That's my way of doing things in the morning—and I love it!

But sometimes we have a way of doing things that is *not* okay. And we may not even be aware of it.

As I walked through the many layers of healing, I began to recognize certain triggers. There were times when my battle with food was much more intense than others. Weekends away from the safety of my home was one of them.

One week, with building anxiety, I approached a weekend away from home—a weekend surrounded by people and food. A heaviness settled over my being.

The stage was set.

Every misplaced emotion inside me was primed and ready to react at the slightest infraction. The feeling is hard to describe. It is like standing on the edge of a precipice, knowing that at any moment something or someone might give you a shove.

It generates an agitation within me. I become extremely wary and uptight. I'm unable to rest because inside me is this coil, ready to spring, like a mousetrap that suddenly SNAPS!

I felt the tension rising within me as the week progressed, each day adding another twist to the already tightly wound coil. I tried to relax, determined to keep my eating disorder tendencies under control—to not let the coil snap.

Then I had a very clear thought: *This battle, this endless routine of always fighting my eating disorder, is simply not okay. Somehow it has to stop.*

Through tears, I made a desperate plea to God for help. "God, how can I do this? How can I safely maneuver through these familiar dangerous pathways and yet stay on the right path? How can I retrain myself to a new routine?"

And God answered with a thought:

No sugar.

What? I was almost sure it was a Sarah thought and not a God thought. But as the day wore on, I became more certain—this was a God thought. This was God's way of changing my focus. It broke through my vicious circle of thoughts and gave me a new incentive. A plan.

As soon as I accepted the thought and prayed, "Okay, Lord, no sugar this weekend," the coil released without its usual snap of reaction. I felt my mind and heart relax.

Wonder of wonders. Would this really work? In awe, I tentatively presented the thought to Hannah, and her tears affirmed that God had spoken to me. In a simple, quiet way, He had come through.

It was such a simple suggestion, almost absurd, yet it was just what I needed. With only two words, God not only showed me a path around my anxiety but also gave me confidence that I could be trusted to restrict something for a short time—without obsessing. It surprised me to be trusted, and this gave me more confidence than I had felt for a long time.

God showed me that by taking control of one area of my weakness, I could navigate the weekend food triggers with success. By choosing beforehand that I would not have sugar, I could tell myself that I had eaten adequately and argue against the thoughts of purging. All through the weekend, I carefully chose my food, avoided sugary things, and marveled at the peace I felt.

> But now God had given me a better way—confess... repent... and wait on Him.

It worked so well. After all, it was God's idea.

If I had gone into my weekend with no plan, my anxieties high and triggered, I would likely have walked away with a relapse. This would have given me another conundrum: Do I share my failure or do I hide it? Eating disorders always want secrecy. And I knew honesty is an absolute necessity for healing.

Part of my peace that weekend came from finally being willing to come to God and say, "How can I do this better?" Always before, I had feared giving everything up because I didn't know what else to do.

Having shrouded this part of my life in lies for so long, this took a lot longer to sift through than I thought it would. There were so many thinking patterns wrapped around the gnarled roots of lies. It was starting to look hopeless.

But now God had given me a better way—confess... repent... and wait on Him.

A top priority in this quest for healing and seeking God is integrity—in every part of my life. I need Him to rid me of all deception, of every desire for it. No matter what comes, I want to live openly and honestly. It's a new way of living, but God can show me how. He's the God of love and mercy.

And good ideas.

Try It MY Way

Mentor's Thoughts

Anorexia and bulimia are not really about food—they are surface manifestations of a deeper issue. As I wrote in the last chapter, we must focus on learning how God intends for us to live and care for our bodies. This includes giving up control and trusting that His ways are best, even when they don't make sense to us.

I recall a story told by a swimming instructor about a man she had tried to teach to swim. He was in the Marines and built like a linebacker—the kind of man you think wouldn't be afraid of anything. But he was petrified of water. The instructor tried to teach him that water was nothing to fear. If we submit to its properties and understand how it works, we will float easily. Only if we fight it will we sink.

But this giant of a man could not believe this. He clung desperately to the side of the pool and fought the water until the instructor finally gave up. The man simply could not relax and submit to the buoyancy of the water. And unless he could do that, he would always be bound by his fear of water.

> It is not about having a life of peace with no conflict—it is about having peace in the midst of conflict.

In the same way, God is calling us to a life of trust and submission to His way of carrying us. If we insist on controlling everything that comes our way, we will always be in bondage to our own safety parameters. Not until we let go and believe that our Father's buoyancy will carry us through will we truly be free.

The idea of giving up control is not highly esteemed in normal society. People think freedom comes from being in control of our world and making others bow to us. They think we need to make walls so no one can hurt us or take advantage of us. We refuse to trust anyone, especially not God. The prevailing thought is that the strongest wins, the smartest rules, and the craftiest is in charge.

But our Father, the One who created us, gives us a different way to live. The world will never understand the power of crucifying self, of walking the second mile, of turning the other cheek. It looks like foolishness.

To that petrified Marine, it seemed foolish to let go and trust what the instructor said. Maybe he had just met her and didn't know if she was reliable.

But we know that our Instructor is reliable. The road ahead may look scary, but when we learn to live close to the Father's heart, we can trust Him to guide us. It is not about having a life of peace with no conflict—it is about having peace in the midst of conflict. And staying near to the heart of God.

The root of eating disorders is not about food. It is about giving up control, about learning to trust God instead of our instincts, about accepting that our perfectionist obsessions are destroying us. It is about being willing to stop fighting, about giving in to the One who knows us better than we know ourselves.

But food can't be ignored. The tendency of someone recovering from anorexia is to flip from being hyper-focused on food to taking all focus off food. *I just won't think about it so I won't obsess,* people think. While this may be needed for a time while resetting wrong thinking patterns, at some point we need to develop a healthy relationship with food. This is true for someone who overeats just as much as for someone who refuses to eat.

Since anorexia is steeped in food obsessions, it may take some time before that is sufficiently healed and a person is able to focus on food again. A lie of anorexia says that unless we maintain tight control, we will lose all constraint and become obese.

In Sarah's journey, it was difficult for her to realize that balanced living means being purposeful about eating healthily. It required being educated about eating foods in the right quantities and about the nutritional value of healthy fats and carbs, things she considered "taboo." It meant discerning the difference between obsessing about food and learning what is needed to stay healthy.

This also reaches into the realm of exercise. Anorexia drives a person to exercise for hours, sometimes to the point of collapse. When a person realizes this is not healthy, the all-or-nothing mindset of perfectionism takes over: "If I can't do that, then I won't exercise at all." But nothing could be further from the truth. Our bodies were designed for activity—lots of it. A sedentary lifestyle usually leads to health issues. We just need a proper balance.

Learning a new way means learning how to discern between obsession and proper focus, between anxiety and trust, between fear and understanding, between lies and truth. God has called us to a purposeful life, one that seeks to understand His ways. It is about pursuing wisdom but leaving control in His hands. It is about trusting even when it looks scary.

Above all, it is getting to know the Father's heart.

Writing Out Your Thoughts...

1. Do you feel a deep fear at the thought of letting go of control? What is one thing you fear letting go of, and what is the worst thing you imagine could happen if you would?

2. What do you think is the difference between obsessing about food and being focused on what you eat?

3. In what ways do you relate to Sarah's need for secrecy? What do you find the most difficult to be open and honest about?

4. Read 1 John 1: 5-7 below. What do you think it means to "walk in the light"? Is there any room for deception if we walk in God's light? What does it mean to "walk in darkness"?

> *This then is the message which we have heard of him, and declare unto you, that God is light, and in him is no darkness at all. If we say that we have fellowship with him, and walk in darkness, we lie, and do not the truth: but if we walk in the light, as he is in the light, we have fellowship one with another, and the blood of Jesus Christ his Son cleanseth us from all sin.* 1 John 1:5-7

chapter 20

Straight Talk

Have you ever had a time in your life when someone got up close and gave you some straight talk? It's often not a very pleasant experience, so I'm guessing if it happened to you, you clearly remember it.

I do. And I'm sure I deserved it.

I'd like to give you a little straight talk now, but not in an "in your face" sort of way. Just straight from my heart to yours. Eye to eye. Very serious.

I'm not upset or shaking my finger at you. What I am about to say is because I care and I understand.

I'm going to share this very honestly, straight from my heart. I have been there, and it usually comes at a time when we are really struggling.

There is one thing Satan likes to hit us with when we are down and fighting a hard battle.

It may come as a whisper... *You should just die. They'd all be better off without you. Why don't you just...?*

When those thoughts come—and they likely will—no matter how small or quiet, my friend, rebuke them!

Suicide is never a good option. People often shy away from this conversation, but I believe with all my heart that exposing a lie takes away its power.

Never believe the lie that suicide is a way out. It is not. This idea comes from the pit of hell, from the devil himself. If you remember this, you will be able to rebuke these thoughts.

God is the Giver of life. He is the One—and the only One—to choose when we leave this world. Any thoughts of death or dying to escape any situation can be traced back to sulfurous breath and evil. Recognize that evil voice. Satan will deceive you into thinking everyone would be better off without you. That is not true. Each of us is important and leaves a mark in this world. Each of our lives touches others.

When Mary was counseling me, she told me in a moment of straight talk that suicide is not an option. It doesn't show you the whole picture. What looks like an escape from pain is a flat out lie.

It can never, ever be an option.

We cannot stop the thoughts that come through our mind, but we have the power to choose which ones remain. Thoughts that circle around suicide are poisonous. They are a deadly, toxic poison. We must immediately rebuke them in the name of Jesus. If all we can do is call on His name—that is enough.

Tell Him to come to you—to save you from these thoughts. He will be right there. Remember, He can always hear your cry for help.

The next step is to tell a safe friend, a family member, or a counselor. Someone like this can help us have victory over these thoughts before they poison our mind. Remember, sharing a burden makes it half the burden.

Do not suffer alone. Stop feeding these thoughts before they take you where you never thought you'd go. And never use suicide as a threat to get what you want. That only makes things worse.

One life lost to suicide is one too many. Just because you grew up in a Christian home or attended church doesn't mean Satan won't try you with these thoughts. He is the accuser of the brethren, and his goal is that you be as lost in despair as he is.

God has a plan for us—and it is not the end until He says so. He is the final authority.

When I was seventeen years old, a young man I knew took his life. If you could have seen the pain etched on his parents' faces...their grief and unanswered questions...and the sick feelings of all who knew him, you would see what suicide really is.

> We cannot stop the thoughts that come through our mind, but we have the power to choose which ones remain.

I know what it's like to be hit out of the blue with a thought like this. But I'd like to think that if I had read a book like this, it may have helped me recognize it sooner for the horrible lie it is.

But enough of this straight talk now. I think you hear my heart.

God has a great plan for us. The journey we are on is just that—a journey. And if we are on a journey, we are going somewhere. Life will not always be the way it is now. Circumstances change.

No matter what you are facing, no matter how much pain, fear, or sadness you have, remember this—*there is always HOPE*. If you turn to the Light, happiness can be found even in the darkest of times.

Never forget that.

Writing Out Your Thoughts...

1. Do you ever feel like there is no reason for living? Name one person who cares about what happens to you. Next, write a short prayer thanking God for that person in your life.

2. Think of the story of Job in the Bible. He was a rich man with many children. List all the bad things that happened to Job.

3. Look up Job 13:15 and copy the verse. What is it telling you?

4. "Integrity" means to have a "firm adherence to a code of especially moral values." How did Job show integrity?

5. How can you show integrity when Satan tempts you with despair and the lie that there is no hope?

6. When Satan tempted Jesus in Matthew 4, he did it by saying, "If…" Jesus did not argue but used God's Word to speak the truth. Satan can never stand against the truth of God's Word. If you find yourself in a deep, dark hole, call on the name of Jesus and use God's Word to quiet the voice of despair. Write out your favorite verses of hope and keep adding to your list. Read them out loud when times get dark and hope seems gone.

> *For he hath said, I will never leave thee, nor forsake thee.* Hebrews 13:5

Chapter 21

Letter of Release

As I walk the journey away from eating disorder thoughts, I am struck with the awareness that so many of these thoughts and patterns took on a twisted form of truth.

And they actually seemed like the truth at the time. As I look at my eating disorder, I can see ways it helped me cope in times of stress, even though it was harmful. Although I have learned better and more helpful ways now, that part of me will always be there. I acknowledge it, just as I acknowledge that a part of me still has the feelings of a lonely little girl.

This area in my life makes up a part of who I am. If I deny it, I am denying the existence of a part of me. It's like denying that your hand exists. Even if you say it doesn't, it is still there.

Part of finding the pathway to healing comes in being willing to accept all the different areas of your experiences and your reactions. You must accept them as part of you.

For me, that means accepting the part of me that always tends to cry. I still cry easily. It is a part of who I am. I may not always like it, but it is the way God made me—and it is okay.

My tears have become such a part of me that my children make comments that make me smile. "Oh, there goes Mom again..." And they roll their eyes good-naturedly at my tears—or give me a hug and join me. I have come to learn that tears can help soften a situation, and I need not be ashamed that God made me this way.

This also means accepting my sensitive and perfectionistic nature. That doesn't mean I allow myself to be easily offended, but I accept that things will touch my heart deeply. I will hurt when I see others hurting, but I will need to remind myself that I am not called to fix all the world's hurts.

> There is beauty in acceptance and peace in surrender.

It doesn't mean I accept the negative ways that perfectionism can pull me down, but I realize my weakness and seek to allow God to temper me into His nature. I must allow myself grace to be who God made me to be—an imperfect mortal.

It also means accepting that I might struggle with food. As a way of acknowledging that part of me, but moving on in freedom, I wrote a letter of release to the eating-disordered part of me. I encourage you to do the same in your area of struggle.

Acknowledge how your addiction may have helped you, albeit negatively, but then say that you do not need it any longer. That God has a better way to deal with life's situations.

Thank you, eating disorder, for the way you helped me cope with food, stress, and confusion in the past. It really did help to numb the strain and pain that went with my personality—my sensitivity and need for perfection. The purging released the extreme stress, and the obsessive eating or restricting made me feel like I had some control in an out-of-control world. The obsessive exercising released in me a feeling of power.

But I don't need that anymore, eating disorder. You see, I have found a way that is more helpful—a way that won't kill me or damage my body. This way is far better. You lied to me, and I have found truth through Jesus.

He wants me to care for my body. He wants me to be healthy, and I can do that and feel way better than you ever made me feel. He wants me to come to Him, not you, for peace and freedom. You are bondage—Jesus is the way of truth and hope and life. My body is not my own—I have been bought with a price.

Goodbye, eating disorder, I don't need you anymore.

With that letter of release, I aimed to put to rest a part of me that still fights for control. I can't deny that it is there, but I can put it in its place.

Under the power of Jesus.

It may always be a part of me, but I don't have to let it take over my life again. It may always be a weakness, but in Christ I am made strong.

There is beauty in acceptance and peace in surrender. There is strength in sorrow for what has been lost, but there is also hope for the future.

I am so grateful for the One who gave His all for me.

Because of Him, I am free.

Letter of Release

Writing Out Your Thoughts...

1. List ways your eating disorder (or other form of bondage) has helped you cope in the past.

2. List ways you are learning to cope in God's way instead.

3. Write your own letter of release to the old ways, admitting how they may have helped you, but explaining how God is now in control of your life.

> *Remember ye not the former things, neither consider the things of old. Behold, I will do a new thing; now it shall spring forth; shall ye not know it? I will even make a way in the wilderness, and rivers in the desert.* Isaiah 43:18-19

chapter 22

Healed?

I love the stories in the Bible where Jesus did so many miracles of healing. I try to imagine how it must have been to be walking with Him and see someone going from paralyzed to leaping for joy!

What an awesome experience.

I have often wished for that—a prayer, a touch, and *zing!* No more battle. Everything I had ever dealt with would be gone. Miraculously.

I believe God could do that. But He usually doesn't, and I see why—at least for me.

It is through the battles that we find true strength.

Am I completely healed? No.

Am I walking in healing? Yes! Praise God, I am! Healing is so much more than I had thought. It does not mean never fighting any battles again—it is seeing them for what they are and learning to cope.

The reason so many people relapse in eating disorders is because they assume they are healed—that it is all behind them. They let down their guard, and it often returns with a vengeance.

It took me a while, but I can now say with joy that I am walking in healing. What does that look like for me?

> It is through the battles that we find true strength.

It is choosing health over being thin. It is making a deliberate choice to eat three healthy meals a day and to exercise responsibly. It means having accountability. It means admitting any serious failures in my thinking about food and asking for help when I battle circular thoughts about my body image.

Healing also means acknowledging when I am sad, hurt, or angry—and being willing to talk about it. It means being real, not pretending. It means truth and integrity, not deception or deceit. It means accepting the things I cannot change and being brave enough to change what I can.

Walking in healing means there are things I know I cannot do. Maybe it is all right for others, but it is not for me. Healing means I rebuke shame in my life, and I face the future with hope and God's Word.

Healing means admitting that there are areas where I am weak and haven't been able to find freedom. Like the scale. At this point, the scale is still too much of a trigger for me, so I am not weighing myself regularly. I stopped because it wasn't working for me. If anything has the power to ruin my day, it has too much power.

Healing means I am willing to gauge my body by the way my clothing fits or doesn't fit—without obsessive body-checking. All I need is a gentle awareness to help me know if I need to eat a little more or maybe a little less.

Will I eventually be able to weigh myself? Maybe. Maybe not. And I need to be okay with that.

That is healing.

Healing means I can look at my past, but it doesn't define me. I do not place blame or remain offended by things that happened to me—whether they are wounds inflicted by others or a result of my own mistakes. These grievances are not mine to deal with—they are God's.

Healing means I can say without anger, "I forgive you." I can also say, "I am sorry." By the grace of God, I have forgiven and am forgiven. Does that mean those things never hurt? No. But walking in healing means I will choose each day to take care of what I can and then move forward. When thoughts of hurt want to settle within me, I will turn them over to God.

We will never walk in healing as long as we blame others for our problems. We must step out of that wounded mentality and move forward to joy, hope, and freedom. God has a beautiful journey before us that is far greater than the hurts we have experienced or are experiencing.

Healing doesn't mean that everything is fixed, and the pain is all covered up. It means that I accept where I am at this time, and that no matter the circumstances, God can handle it. It means I accept my personality as God made me, and I let Him make me more Christlike in the areas that are not okay.

Healing means I can thank God for my culture and my heritage, even if things aren't perfect. Too many wounded people look for a place to throw blame. "If this is Christianity, I want nothing to do with it... If this is the way the Mennonite/Amish/Baptist/Pentecostal churches are, then I want no part of them..." If I cannot look back and thank God for what He has allowed in my past, I will never truly have peace going forward.

Just because we may be wounded by the broken people within our circles doesn't mean the entire culture is bad. Be careful in your walk to healing that you don't place a label upon the very community God meant for you to be a part of. Don't throw it out just because you were hurt or wounded, but seek God in prayer earnestly before you make a move you may someday regret.

I'm not saying it is never God's will for someone to leave one culture for another, but let's examine our motives deeply. Romans 1:21 says, "Because that, when they knew God, they glorified him not as God, neither were thankful." We must be thankful for our past, our present, and our future.

> Healing is a way of life, not an instantaneous moment.

Healing means *His* way—not mine. I am being healed not because of great things I have done, but because I reached out and touched the hem of His garment.

And I will not let go.

His healing power is for you too, my friend. Reach out and touch His garment.

Healing means understanding that God is our Father, and we are His children. He loves us and has planned a life of freedom for us.

The steps we take to healing can be milestones on our journey to the sanctuary—the place right next to God's heart. The place of peace and rest. Don't put boundaries on what you think your healing might be like. Just take one step at a time. One moment at a time.

I don't think I'll ever be able to say I am totally healed until the day I place my hand in His and He pulls me into His embrace. At that blessed moment, His nail-scarred hands will gather me up, and I will never, ever wander again.

The day I step over the threshold into heaven and see the face of my Savior—that will be the day He truly marks me healed. Healed by the blood of the Lamb. Every valley, every battle, every negative and traumatic experience will then be worth it all.

Healing is a way of life, not an instantaneous moment. Because of this, it's the best experience I've ever had. I have moved from empty and hollow to filled with a glorious hope.

Fight on. The battle is not ours, but God's!

Mentor's Thoughts

I glanced at the instructions to make the outdoor swing seat, then I looked at the finished one that was there for us to see how it should look when we were done. Even though I did a lot of sewing, I was puzzled. I was helping my daughter and the others in her sewing class put their swing seats together, but it didn't make sense.

The class teacher finally told me to just read the instructions and follow them step by step. So we started with step one (which I was sure was wrong) and proceeded one step at a time. Gradually it started coming together—and making sense! I could see it was going to work.

Because I followed the instructions, we took home a lovely and comfortable outdoor swing seat. If I had insisted on doing it my way, it would have been a failure.

I needed to trust the instructions.

We need to do the same in the journey of healing. When we first agree to walk with God in the way He has for us, we may have an idea what our healing must look like. But our Father says, "I know you better than you know yourself. Leave the details in my hands and just walk in trust and obedience."

Trust is the hardest thing He will ever ask of us, and yet it is the only way we will ever be free. We want God to take us around the hard and painful places, but He is calling us to walk through them. He knows that the only way to freedom may be through our pain and shame, though that makes little sense to us and does not seem safe.

Although safety is a gift from God, it often becomes an idol. Our Father wants us to seek our safety only in Him. This may feel wrong at times, but we must trust our Instructor.

The world and the devil have distorted the way we understand our Father and His ways. Too often we feel that to be a good Christian, we must look the right way, act the right way, and say the right things. This is true if those "right" things are what God's Word tells us to do, but so often our performance is based on what other people think or say we should do.

What does Christian living mean to us? Do we believe we are able to follow Christ in a way that pleases Him and that we can be approved by a holy God? Or do we look to the "giants" of faith and feel inadequate? Is it possible that these Bible heroes also felt weak and unable? The poem on page 222 gives us a true picture of Christianity.

Satan's lies of perfectionism would have us believe that God's standards are impossible to accomplish. He wants us to become distracted by trying to reach unattainable goals that God never meant for us to achieve on our own. He sent Jesus to make a way for the smallest, weakest sinner to become His beloved child. He is not asking perfection of us.

He just wants a humble, surrendered heart.

Writing Out Your Thoughts...

1. If you could choose any miracle of instant healing, what would it be? Can you think of reasons why God may not choose to heal you in this way? In what ways does a difficult journey make you stronger than instant healing would?

2. What do you think the difference is between being "healed" and "walking in healing"?

3. What do you think "walking in healing" might look like in your own life?

4. Can you accept that nothing in this world is perfect except God? Does admitting your weakness make you feel ashamed? Why? How do you think God sees your weakness?

> **SERENITY PRAYER**
> *God, grant me the serenity to accept the things I cannot change, the courage to change the things I can, and the wisdom to know the difference.*

When I Say I'm a Christian

When I say, "I am a Christian"
I'm not shouting, "I've been saved!"
I'm whispering, "I get lost sometimes
That's why I chose this way"

When I say, "I am a Christian"
I don't speak with human pride
I'm confessing that I stumble—
Needing God to be my guide

When I say, "I am a Christian"
I'm not trying to be strong
I'm professing that I'm weak
and pray for strength to carry on

When I say, "I am a Christian"
I'm not bragging of success
I'm admitting that I've failed
and cannot ever pay the debt

When I say, "I am a Christian"
I don't think I know it all
I submit to my confusion
asking humbly to be taught

When I say, "I am a Christian"
I'm not claiming to be perfect
My flaws are far too visible
but God believes I'm worth it

When I say, "I am a Christian"
I still feel the sting of pain
I have my share of heartache
which is why I seek God's name.

When I say, "I am a Christian"
I do not wish to judge
I have no authority
I only know I'm loved

© 1988 Carol Wimmer. Used by permission.

Closing Letter

Dear friend,

Thank you so much for taking the time to read my journey to God's heart. My prayer is that you are longing for a closer walk with God. He is a good, good Father—look for Him and you will find Him.

I wish I could sit down and hear your story. I would cry with you and listen as you share your pain and your struggles. I'd make you tea or coffee and we'd talk.

I know I can't reach out to everyone, but my God can. It is so amazing. He can connect hearts in ways we can't imagine.

Years ago I had a dream... It was unlike any other dream I've ever had. I woke up, not with a picture in my mind, but rather a feeling—a feeling of awe, reverence, and peace. It was so overwhelming that, you guessed it, I cried... And with that feeling came a verse, so clear in my mind that it made the hair on my arms and neck prickle.

It was part of Revelation 7:14: "These are they which came out of great tribulation, and have washed their robes, and made them white in the blood of the Lamb." Since that verse was in my head like a voice, I immediately looked it up and read the whole chapter. Like a comforting whisper, the words washed over me.

Who are those with white robes around the throne praising God day and night in His temple? Who are those who shall neither hunger nor thirst anymore? Who are those who need neither the sun nor the moon?

They are those who have come through great tribulation and have washed their robes and made them white in the blood of the Lamb! That promise is for you and for me. It's a future glimpse of God's children—all safely Home. They have overcome the wicked one by the blood of the Lamb.

That dream and those words gave me so much hope.

The end of that chapter, at least to me, is ironically beautiful. Look at verse 17 (emphasis mine): "For the Lamb which is in the midst of the throne *shall feed them,* and shall lead them unto living fountains of waters…" If that reference to God feeding us doesn't make you smile (especially now that you know my story) look at the end of that verse: *"…and God shall wipe away all tears from their eyes."*

No more tears. Do you understand now that He is a personal God?

Oh, my friend, He is! And He wants to be personal with you.

I leave you now with this: Seek God. Make your salvation sure. Call His name. He has a healing for you like you cannot imagine. Be strong and courageous. You can have victory. Hold tightly to His hand.

There is hope and a future for you—beyond the pain.

Let us press on together. Though we may never meet here on earth, I want to meet you up there around that beautiful throne—in the presence of our SAVIOR, the true Healer.

Because He lives,

Sarah

Resources

Note: Although we found the following listed resources helpful, some may contain information we are not in full agreement with. Use prayerful discernment.

ONLINE:

- Cuncic, Arlin. "The Psychology of Shame." https://www.verywellmind.com/what-is-shame-5115076.

- Norberg, Grace. "Challenging Perfectionism." https://www.symmetrycounseling.com/uncategorized/challenging-perfectionism/.

- Rittenhouse, Margot. "Anorexia Nervosa Experiencing Hunger and Fullness." https://www.eatingdisorderhope.com/blog/anorexia-nervosa-hunger-fullness.

- Scott, Elizabeth. "Are You a Highly Sensitive Person?" https://www.verywellmind.com/highly-sensitive-persons-traits-that-create-more-stress-4126393.

- "What Are the Effects of Diuretic Misuse?" Eating Disorders Online. https://www.eatingdisordersonline.com/medical/diuretics.php.

- Witmer, Asher. "The Secret to Healthy Accountability." https://asherwitmer.com/the-secret-to-healthy-accountability/.

BOOKS:

- Allender, Dan. *When Trust Is Lost: Healing for Victims of Sexual Abuse.* RBC Ministries, Grand Rapids, MI, 2010.

- Brown, Harriet. *Brave Girl Eating: A Family's Struggle With Anorexia.* HarperCollins Publishers, New York, NY, 2011.

- Claude-Pierre, Peggy. *The Secret Language of Eating Disorders: How You Can Understand and Work to Cure Anorexia and Bulimia.* Vintage Books/Random House, New York, NY, 1997.

- Cooperman, Sheila & Gilbert, Sara. *Living With Eating Disorders.* Checkmark Books, New York, NY, 2009.

- Costin, Carolyn. *The Eating Disorder Sourcebook: A Comprehensive Guide to the Causes, Treatment, and Prevention of Eating Disorders,* 3rd ed. McGraw-Hill, New York, NY, 2007.

- Costin, Carolyn & Grabb, Gwen S. *8 Keys to Recovery From an Eating Disorder: Effective Strategies From Therapeutic Practice and Personal Experience.* W.W. Norton & Company, New York, NY, 2011.

- Cruse, Sheryle. *Thin Enough: My Spiritual Journey Through the Living Death of an Eating Disorder.* New Hope Publishers, Birmingham, AL, 2006

- Delony, Dr. John. *Redefining Anxiety.* Ramsey Press, Franklin, TN, 2020.

- DeMuth, Mary E. *Thin Places: A Memoir.* Zondervan, Grand Rapids, MI, 2010.

- Goulston, Mark. *Post-Traumatic Stress Disorder for Dummies.* Wiley Publishing, Inc., Hoboken, NJ, 2008.

- Gresh, Dannah & Wolgemuth, Nancy D. *Lies Girls Believe & the Truth That Sets Them Free.* Versa Press, East Peoria, IL, 2019.

- Heaton, Jeanne A. & Strauss, Claudia J. *Talking to Eating Disorders: Simple Ways to Support Someone With Anorexia, Bulimia, or Other Eating Disorders.* Penguin Group, New York, NY, 2005.

- Hunt, June. *Anorexia & Bulimia: Control That Is Out of Control.* Aspire Press, Torrance, CA, 2014.

- Jantz, Gregory L. with McMurray, Ann. *Hope, Help & Healing for Eating Disorders: A Whole-Person Approach to Treatment of Anorexia, Bulimia, and Disordered Eating.* WaterBrook Press, Colorado Springs, CO, 2010.

- Liu, Aimee. *Gaining: The Truth About Life After Eating Disorders.* Warner Books, New York, NY, 2007.

- Morrow, Jena. *Hollow: An Unpolished Tale.* Moody Publishers, Chicago, IL, 2010.

- Morrow, Jena. *Hope for the Hollow: A Thirty-Day Inside-Out Makeover for Women Recovering From Eating Disorders.* Lighthouse Publishing of the Carolinas, Birmingham, AL, 2013.

- Rumney, Avis. *Dying To Please: Anorexia, Treatment and Recovery*, 2nd ed. McFarland & Co., Jefferson, NC, 2009.

- Shaw, Mark E., with Bailey, Rachel & Spence, Bethany. *Eating Disorders: Hope for Hungering Souls*. Focus Publishing, Bemidji, MN, 2014.

- Tripp, Paul D. *Instruments in the Redeemer's Hand*. P&R Publishing, Phillipsburg, NJ, 2002.

- Van der Kolk, Bessel. *The Body Keeps the Score: Brain, Mind, and Body in the Healing of Trauma*. Penguin Books, New York, NY, 2014.

- Wierenga, Emily T. *Chasing Silhouettes: How to Help a Loved One Battling an Eating Disorder*. Ampelon Publishing, Boise, ID, 2012.

About Christian Aid Ministries

Christian Aid Ministries was founded in 1981 as a nonprofit, tax-exempt 501(c)(3) organization. Its primary purpose is to provide a trustworthy and efficient channel for Amish, Mennonite, and other conservative Anabaptist groups and individuals to minister to physical and spiritual needs around the world. This is in response to the command to "Do good unto all men, especially unto them who are of the household of faith" (Galatians 6:10).

CAM supporters provide millions of pounds of food, clothing, Bibles, medicines, and other aid each year. Supporters' funds also help victims of disasters in the U.S. and abroad, put up Gospel billboards in the U.S., and provide Biblical teaching and self-help resources. CAM's main purposes for providing aid are to help and encourage God's people and bring the Gospel to a lost and dying world.

The Way to God and Peace

We live in a world contaminated by sin. Sin is anything that goes against God's holy standards. When we do not follow the guidelines that God our Creator gave us, we are guilty of sin. Sin separates us from God, the source of life.

Since the time when the first man and woman, Adam and Eve, sinned in the Garden of Eden, sin has been universal. The Bible says that we all have "sinned and come short of the glory of God" (Romans 3:23). It also says that the natural consequence for that sin is eternal death, or punishment in an eternal hell: "Then when lust hath conceived, it bringeth forth sin: and sin, when it is finished, bringeth forth death" (James 1:15).

But we do not have to suffer eternal death in hell. God provided forgiveness for our sins through the death of His only Son, Jesus Christ. Because Jesus was perfect and without sin, He could die in our place. "For God so loved the world that he gave his only begotten Son, that whosoever believeth in him should not perish, but have everlasting life" (John 3:16).

A sacrifice is something given to benefit someone else. It costs the giver greatly. Jesus was God's sacrifice. Jesus' death takes away the penalty of sin for all those who accept this sacrifice and truly repent of their sins. To repent of sins means to be truly sorry for and turn away from the things we have done that have violated God's standards (Acts 2:38; 3:19).

Jesus died, but He did not remain dead. After three days, God's Spirit miraculously raised Him to life again. God's Spirit does something similar in us. When we receive Jesus as our sacrifice and repent of our sins, our hearts are changed. We become spiritually alive! We develop new desires and attitudes (2 Corinthians 5:17). We begin to make choices that please God (1 John 3:9). If we do fail and commit sins, we can ask God for forgiveness. "If we confess our sins, he is faithful and just to forgive us our sins, and to cleanse us from all unrighteousness" (1 John 1:9).

Once our hearts have been changed, we want to continue growing spiritually. We will be happy to let Jesus be the Master of our lives and will want to become more like Him. To do this, we must meditate on God's Word and commune with God in prayer. We will testify to others of this change by being baptized and sharing the good news of God's victory over sin and death. Fellowship with a faithful group of believers will strengthen our walk with God (1 John 1:7).